READER'S DIGEST

HOW TO DO
just about
ANYTHING IN
Microsoft®
Word

Published by The Reader's Digest Association Limited
London • New York • Sydney • Montreal

How to do just about anything in Microsoft® Word

was edited and designed by The Reader's Digest Association Limited, London

First edition Copyright ©2001
The Reader's Digest Association Limited,
11 Westferry Circus, Canary Wharf, London E14 4HE.
www.readersdigest.co.uk

We are committed to both the quality of our products and the service we provide to our customers.
We value your comments, so please feel free to contact us on **08705 113366**,
or by email at **cust_service@readersdigest.co.uk**
If you have any comments or suggestions about this book, e-mail us at: **gbeditorial@readersdigest.co.uk**

Printed in China
ISBN 0 276 42588 X

HOW TO DO
just about
ANYTHING IN
Microsoft®
Word

PLANET THREE PUBLISHING NETWORK

Edited, designed and produced by
Planet Three Publishing Network
Northburgh House, 10 Northburgh Street,
London EC1V 0AT

Editors
Eva Lauer
Gordon Torbet

Subeditors
Alan Brookes
Mary O'Sullivan
Jennifer Patterson
Mary Pickles
Laura Ward

Commissioning Editor
Jon Asbury

Art Editors
Gary Gilbert
Paula Keogh
Andrew Thomas
Michael Yeowell

Contributor
Lindy Newton

For Reader's Digest
Editor
Caroline Boucher

Art Editor
Julie Bennett

Reader's Digest General Books
Editorial Director
Cortina Butler

Art Director
Nick Clark

Executive Editor
Julian Browne

Development Editor
Ruth Binney

Publishing Projects Manager
Alastair Holmes

Style Editor
Ron Pankhurst

Contents

Basics

Styling Your Document

Styling Your Text

Editing Text

Customising Word

Using Graphics

Special Functions

How to use this book

This book is a fun and approachable guide to mastering Microsoft Word. All the most useful features of the program are clearly set out as step-by-step projects, with pictures that show you exactly what you will see on screen. Unlike a manual, you'll never find yourself wondering how to complete a task or having to unravel complicated instructions.

GETTING AROUND THE BOOK

This book covers the main features of Word. You can either read it from start to finish, or dip in and out, as you wish.

Basics
Are you completely new to Word? Learn how to create, save and print your first ever document.

Customising Word
Word's automatic settings dictate how you work. Find out how to set your own preferences.

Styling text
You can style text to suit all kinds of documents, from formal letters to party invitations. Discover the typefaces and how to size and style them.

Styling your document
Word is an extremely versatile program. Learn how to make your newsletter look professional, use columns of text, set indents on paragraphs, create stylish borders and lots more.

Editing text
With just a few key strokes, you can select and move whole paragraphs of text, and search for and replace words or phrases. Thanks to Word's spellchecker and thesaurus, you can also ensure that your documents are always word perfect.

Using graphics
A picture can be worth a thousand words. Using colour, ClipArt, photos and other graphic features, make your documents even more inviting to read.

Special functions
Welcome to the Word masterclass! Here you can find out how to do some of the more challenging tasks, such as creating mail merges or Web pages. These fun and useful functions are simpler than you might expect.

WHICH VERSION OF WORD?
The information in this book is based on a PC using Word 2000. If you have Word 97, you'll find that it looks different to Word 2000, but the functions explained in these pages are very similar or even identical.

Close up
These project-related tips offer you extra detail on various Word functions.

Key word
You'll find handy definitions of technical words or phrases here.

Bright idea
Wondering how to use your new-found skills? Look out for these tips.

GETTING AROUND THE PAGE

You're guided through every task in this book by means of illustrated steps and a range of visual features. Here are the key elements to look for on each page.

Before you start

Projects begin with a small section of text to read. This outlines points to consider and anything you need to do before you begin.

Snapshots

Pictures of the PC screen – 'snapshots' – show you what you'll see on your own screen at each stage of the project.

Annotations

Sometimes a specific part of a step-by-step will be focused on and explained in greater depth.

Magnifications

Snapshots of the PC screen that require special attention are magnified so that you can see them more clearly.

Type in quotes

Words inside quotation marks are either the exact words you will see on screen, or what you need to type in yourself as part of a step.

See also

Want to find out more? This panel points you towards other relevant projects for you to try.

Step-by-step

Projects are set out in clear steps. You are instructed on the keyboard and mouse commands to give, and which files and menus to access.

Useful tips

Near the main block of text are explanations of the more complex aspects of a task and alternative ways to do things.

Bold type

Any bold text is a command for you to carry out. You might need to select a menu option, a toolbar button, a dialogue box tab or press a key.

Page turns

The yellow arrow indicates that your project continues over the page. The features in this book range from two pages to six.

Watch out

These tips will warn you of things to look out for that can cause a project to go wrong, and give advice on how to avoid them.

Expert advice

Advanced tips and guidance to enable you to get professional looking results from all of Word's facilities.

That's amazing!

Inspiring ideas and explanations, such as time-saving shortcuts, which you will find both interesting and useful.

Set up your PC safely

When you are choosing where you want to put your PC, check that there is adequate space and several mains sockets for all the equipment. You need to consider lighting and seating, and the amount of desk space available. If you want to send faxes from your computer or connect to the Internet, you will also need to be near a telephone wall socket.

SITTING AT YOUR COMPUTER

You need to think carefully about how to arrange your area, as a poorly laid out computer desk and PC will be irritating and may prevent you from using your computer properly.

If you find yourself leaning towards the monitor, increase the scale at which you are viewing your document.

Your legs should remain uncrossed and your knees should be lower than your hips.

An adjustable chair will support your back and can be altered to suit each family user.

Your feet should rest flat on the floor.

15°

Your eyes should be at a 15° angle to the centre of the screen

Your desk should be a comfortable height for typing, with your upper arms parallel to your body and your lower arms parallel to the floor.

NAMING AND PLACING PARTS

Your PC's hardware comprises all the parts that you can actually see and handle. Knowing exactly where to place these elements ensures a safe and efficient work area.

Monitor
This houses the computer screen. Position your monitor to avoid reflections, but do not face a bright window yourself as this may lead to eyestrain.

System unit
This is the part of your computer that connects everything together. Leave space so that you can plug in the cables easily and to allow for ventilation. Don't leave cables trailing.

External speakers
For the best sound quality, speakers should be well spaced apart at desk level or higher, not just pushed under the desk. Ensure that the computer is situated so that others are not disturbed by computer games or alert sounds.

Mouse
Place the mouse to the side of your keyboard that suits whether you are left- or right-handed. Use a mouse mat to create the correct amount of friction for the mouse, and be sure there is plenty of room to move the mouse.

Keyboard
Make sure the keyboard is on a stable and level surface within easy reach. Leave enough space in front for hands and wrists. Ensure that the desk is at the correct height.

Printer
Position your printer near the system unit. Make sure there is sufficient space around it for loading the paper trays.

Expert advice
If you are planning to use your computer a lot, either surfing the Internet or doing your accounts and letters, then you should invest in a good quality comfortable office chair. Most dining chairs do not offer the support for your back that is so important when you are sitting still for long periods. Also, most office chairs are adjustable, so it will suit every member of the family. Remember, even with a comfortable chair, you should take regular 10 minute breaks to walk around.

What is Word?

Word processors are programs that enable you to create, save and print documents. Once you have created a document, you can re-use it as often as you like, making any changes and corrections you wish. Word is one of the most versatile word processors available. It makes editing and styling your documents quick, easy and fun.

SEE ALSO...
- *Explore the program* p 16
- *Entering text* p 20
- *Style your text* p 30
- *Edit a toolbar* p 68

WHAT YOU CAN DO

Word offers you an impressive range of options to help make your documents look good and save you time.

Choose from a wide range of typefaces, known as 'fonts', which you can set in different sizes, styles – such as bold, italic or underline – and colours. You can even use special effects, so the text sparkles or flashes, for example.

Design your page

You can set your document to the page size that suits you, choose the size of the margins, how text is aligned, and whether you want it in columns. You can insert boxes and tables, set paragraph indents, and add bullet points or automatically number lists. If you want to illustrate your text, there is a huge library of ClipArt available, or you can insert your own illustrations and photographs.

Work faster with templates

If you're not so keen on setting up documents from scratch, try using Word's ready-made templates instead. These include letterheads, memos, faxes and Web page templates.

Word perfect

Word's Spelling and Grammar facility alerts you to misspelt words and badly constructed sentences. If you're stuck for an alternative word, try using the Thesaurus.

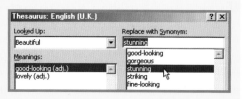

Saving time

If you need to do a mail shot, the Mail Merge facility is a must. Create your letter with gaps for information, such as names and addresses, then merge the letter with data records created in Word or imported from a database.

Word and the Office suite

Although you can buy Word 2000 as a separate program, it usually comes as one of a suite of programs, collectively named 'Microsoft Office'. The software programs bundled in Office vary, depending on which version you buy. The basic version – 'Microsoft Office for Small Businesses' – includes Excel, which is a spreadsheet program, and Outlook, an information management program that also allows you to send and receive e-mails. The more expensive 'Office Professional' also includes PowerPoint for creating on-screen presentations with sound and animation, and Access, a powerful database package.

GETTING AROUND IN WORD

If this is your first time using a word processing program, you'll need a few tips to get you started.

Using the mouse

You use the mouse to point at different areas of the screen and to issue commands. It is designed to sit comfortably under your hand, with your index finger poised over the left button. You will mostly click with the left button, but sometimes you'll need to use the right. When you are following the instructions in this book, 'clicking' the mouse refers to the left button. If you need to use the right, you'll be told to 'right-click'.

When you move the mouse over text on screen, it changes from a white selection arrow

to the insertion point, which looks like a capital I (see left). If you want to enter text, click the insertion point where you want it and type. To select a button on a toolbar or a menu at the top of the screen, point the selection arrow and click.

Double-clicking the left mouse button is a speedy way to select and confirm an option.

Selecting text

To select a whole line of text, position the arrow over the white area on the left of your document,

Moving around the page

You can scroll through your document by clicking on the arrows at either end of the scroll bars to the right and along the bottom of the screen, or by dragging the grey block on the scroll bar up or down.

To select more or less than one line, left-click in front next to your chosen line, and left-click once. It will be highlighted instantly. To select more, or less, than one line, left-click in front of the first character and, with the button held down, drag the mouse over the text as far up, down, left or right as you require. Release the button when you have selected all the text you want. This is known as 'click and drag'.

To select just one word, double-click on it with your left mouse button. If you click three times,

you select the whole paragraph. Once you have selected an area of text, you can style it, change font or font size, copy and paste it into another part of the document, or delete it.

Menus, toolbars and commands

You can issue instructions in three ways - using menus, using the toolbars or using shortcut keys.
Menus: If you're new to Word, it's a good idea to use the menus until you are more familiar with the program (see page 18). The menus are at the

very top of the window, and from them you can style, save and print your document, among other things.

Toolbars: Some of the most common commands appear as buttons on the toolbars. Although they provide a quick route to the same end result, such as aligning or emboldening your selected text, and saving or opening a new document, they do not offer the flexibility of the menu alternatives, which often open up dialogue boxes containing a wider variety of options (see page 18).

Key commands: Shortcut keys are a combination of two or three keystrokes and are useful for people who prefer using the keyboard to the mouse (see overleaf).

Close up
Using Word 2000, you can open a document that has been created in an older version of Word. However, you cannot use an older version of Word to open a document created in Word 2000.

USING THE KEYBOARD

Function keys are shortcuts to commands:
F1 accesses Microsoft Help and Support.
F2 is for moving text. Select your text, press **F2**, click the point on your page where you wish the text to go to and press the **Return** key.
F4 repeats your last command.

F5 opens a dialogue box for 'Find' and 'Replace' features, and 'Go To', which enables you to jump to another part of your document.
F7 checks a document for spelling and grammar.
F12 Creates a duplicate version of your document using the 'Save As' feature.

Insert allows you to type over existing text.
Delete gets rid of any selected text or item.
Home places the cursor at the start of the line.
End places the cursor at the end of the line.
Page Up places the cursor at the top of the page.
Page Down places the cursor at the page bottom.

Caps Lock causes all the letters that you type to appear as capitals.
Shift allows you to type a letter on a key as a capital or to select the topmarked option on the key. For example, pressing 'Shift' + '5' types the '%' symbol.
Ctrl and **Alt** keys, when pressed in conjunction with other keys, access different commands (keyboard shortcuts). For example, 'Ctrl' + 'P' displays the 'Print' dialogue box.
Ctrl + Alt + Delete is a useful way to quit Word, should your screen freeze up.
Windows key Accesses the Start menu.

Spacebar adds spaces between words.

Return creates a paragraph break or ends a line early.

Backspace deletes text to the left of your cursor.

Arrow keys move the cursor up, down, left and right.

Enter key works like the Return key.

Keyboard shortcuts

You can use all kinds of shortcuts to style your text, format your pages and access commands

Ctrl + Shift + Spacebar creates a non-breaking space. This means that the words either side of the space are kept together on the same line.
Ctrl + Shift + hyphen creates a non-breaking hyphen. This means that a hyphenated word will not be split over two lines.
Ctrl + Q removes paragraph formatting.
Ctrl + Spacebar removes character formatting.
Ctrl + B makes text bold.
Ctrl + U underlines text.
Ctrl + I italicises text.
Ctrl + Shift + < decreases font size.
Ctrl + Shift + > increases font size.
Ctrl + F2 previews how your page will look when it is printed.
Ctrl + F4 closes the window you're working in.
Ctrl + F6 goes to the next open Word window.
Alt + F4 closes the Word program.
Alt + F8 runs a pre-recorded macro.
Alt + F10 maximises the Word window.

Close up
Use the Help menu to find out more about Word's function keys and shortcuts using Alt and Ctrl. Click the question mark icon on the toolbar and type in 'keyboard shortcuts'. Click Search.

Basics

Explore the program

Many people use Word more frequently than other programs. Although Word is designed to be intuitive, you will be able to use it more confidently and efficiently if you first take time to get to know the functions in the main document window. This will provide you with a better understanding of the many powerful features on offer.

SEE ALSO...

● *What is Word?* p 12
● *Entering text* p 20

BEFORE YOU START
You may have a shortcut for accessing Word on your computer Desktop. Look out for a 'Word' icon, with a small arrow in the bottom left-hand corner. Double-click on this to run Word.

1 If you don't have a Desktop shortcut to Word, click on the **Start** button, and move the pointer up the menu to highlight **Programs**. The main 'Programs' menu appears. Click on **Microsoft Word** to run it.

2 As the program opens, you will see a title window appear briefly (below). It tells you which version of Word you are using. After a few seconds this window disappears.

3 Next, a blank Word document appears on screen, into which you can start typing text. However, before you do this it is best to become acquainted with the window and the tools that you might want to use to manipulate your text.

THE DOCUMENT WINDOW

**Commands for manipulating text and documents are
listed on drop-down menus or presented as icons on
buttons in the toolbars. Often there are different ways
of accessing the same command.**

Maximize/Restore button
This button enlarges the
window, so it fills the
screen. After maximising,
the button looks like two
overlapping boxes. Click
again to restore the
window to its previous size.

Close buttons
The upper button
closes the program.
The lower button
closes the current
document, but
leaves the Word
program running.

Minimize button
Click here to reduce your document
to a named button on the Taskbar
at the bottom of the screen (see
'Minimized' button below).

Title bar
Shows the name of the document
in which you are working.

Menu bar
Drop-down menus of themed
commands.

Standard toolbar
One-click buttons to activate
common commands.

Formatting toolbar
Buttons and drop-down
menus for formatting text.

Ruler
Shows you the width of your text
area and any indents or tabs you
have set. You can also change these
settings by clicking and sliding the
small tabs along the ruler.

View buttons
Click on these to view your
document in different formats, such
as how it will look when it's printed
or in a Web page format.

Cursor
The flashing cursor,
or 'insertion point',
appears at the start
of a new document
to show you where
text will be inserted

Scroll bars
Use the up and down
arrows to scroll up and
down your document. You
can also click and drag the
grey block up or down, to
move quickly through
multiple page documents

Double arrows buttons
Click here to view the previous page (up
arrows) or the following page (down arrows)

Taskbar
Contains the Start button and
many useful shortcuts to your
programs and settings.

Status bar
Shows the current status of your document. It tells
you which page you are viewing and how many
pages your document contains. It displays where
you are on a page in centimetres, lines and columns.

'Minimized' button
Shows which other documents are
currently open. Here, 'Laura's to do list'
has been minimised. Click on the button
to restore the document.

THE MENU BAR

All the tasks you could want to perform in Word are listed on drop-down menus under the headings on the Menu bar.

File Edit View Insert Format Tools Table Window Help

Before you start using Word, it's a good idea to click on each heading to familiarise yourself with the options. Some actions have icons beside them representing how the command buttons are displayed on the toolbars.

File

Commands in the File menu relate to the management of documents as a whole. Selecting 'New' creates a new document. You can also save, print and quickly open documents that you have recently worked on.

Edit

The Edit menu lists features that allow you to add, move and remove content in a document. You can cut and copy highlighted text and paste it elsewhere in a document. 'Find' will do a search for words and phrases in a document. The 'Undo' command lets you retrace changes you've made and literally undo them.

View

This menu contains commands which allow you to change how you view documents on screen and to see what they look like when they are printed, as well as to zoom in to see more detail or just to make it easier on your eyes. You can also insert headers and footers in your documents from here.

Format

This menu lists options for changing text – either individual letters or whole sections of text. You can alter paragraph settings, change the font and colour of the text and add borders. You can also select a preset style for your whole document.

Tools

The Tools menu offers functions such as checking the spelling and grammar in your text. You can print envelopes using addresses from the contacts section of Microsoft Outlook. You can also customise buttons on the various toolbars from this menu.

Help

If you need help with Word or would like the friendly Office Assistant to help with a specific task, then select the option you want from this menu, including help on the Web.

Expert advice

If you aren't sure what all the icons on your PC mean, go to the **View** menu and select **Toolbars** then **Customise**. Click the **Options** tab. In the 'Other' section, tick the boxes 'Show ScreenTips on toolbars' and 'Show shortcut keys in ScreenTips'. Now, whenever you pass the pointer over an icon the ScreenTip will tell you what it does and what the keyboard shortcut is.

Close up

A double-headed arrow at the bottom of a menu means that further options are available. An arrow to the right of a command in any menu indicates a sub-menu of options. Click on either and the menu will extend.

THE STANDARD TOOLBAR

You will usually see this immediately below the Menu bar of your document. It contains a standardised set of useful command button icons which you can customise, adding the commands that you use frequently.

New Document · Save · Print · Spelling and Grammar · Cut · Paste · Redo Typing · Insert Hyperlink · Insert Table · Create Columns · Show Document Map · Zoom · Word Help

Open Folder · E-mail · Print Preview · Copy · Format Painter · Undo Typing · View Tables and Borders toolbar · Insert an Excel Worksheet · View Drawing toolbar · Show/Hide invisibles · More buttons. Add/Remove buttons

THE FORMATTING TOOLBAR

Below the Standard toolbar in your document window you will usually see the Formatting toolbar. This contains a standardised set of useful command buttons.

Style options · Font Size · Bold · Underline · Center · Align Right · Numbering · Decrease Indent · Outside Border · Font Color

Font · Italic · Align Left · Justify · Bullets · Increase Indent · Highlight · More buttons. Add/Remove buttons

Expert advice

You can create a new document via the Standard toolbar, or via the File menu. The File menu method gives you a choice of templates. You can select just a 'Blank Document' or you can choose from letters, faxes, reports, legal pleadings and so on. The Templates Wizard takes you step-by-step through procedures, such as writing a CV or creating an agenda.

Bright idea

If you make a mistake, just click the Undo *button on the 'Standard' toolbar to rectify it. You can even go back in stages, until you get to a point where you were happy with your document.*

Entering text

Type in your text and you will see it appear on the page of the open document. Unlike typing on a typewriter, you do not have to press the 'Return' key at the end of each line, as the text will automatically flow on to the next line. It doesn't matter if you make mistakes, as you can edit your work at any point, deleting text or moving it around the page.

SEE ALSO...
- *What is Word?* p 12
- *Explore the program* p 16
- *Spelling and grammar* p 58

BEFORE YOU START
Open a document by going to the **File** menu and selecting **New**, then double- click the **Blank Document** icon. Alternatively, click the white **New Blank Document** icon on the toolbar.

1 When you open a document, the cursor always appears at the very beginning of the first page. In a new document, you will start here. Press the **Return** key to insert line spaces and move the cursor down the page until you arrive at the place where you want to start typing. Then start typing your text.

2 In Word, text flows or 'wraps' automatically onto the next line when you reach the right-hand margin. You only need to press the Return key to start a new paragraph, or end a line early, or when making a list.

Click the **Show/Hide** button on the toolbar to reveal or hide non-printing characters, such as returns and spaces.

Expert advice
The keys on your computer's keyboard have different functions and different names. Some, such as the 'Shift' key, need to be held down while you press another key. Others, such as the 'Caps Lock' key, are known as toggle switches: press them once and they are switched on; press them again and they are switched off. The function keys (F1 to F12) are above the standard letter and number keys. These are used for keyboard commands.

Close up
Word can check spelling and grammar for you. A wavy red line appears under misspelt or unrecognisable words. Text that it thinks is grammatically incorrect is marked by a wavy green line.

4 To type a capital letter, hold down the **Shift** key and press the letter key. Shift also causes the upper symbol on a key with two symbols, to be typed. For example, press **Shift + 5** to type '%'. If you want to type a series of capital letters, press the **Caps Lock** key. A green light on the right of your keyboard reminds you the lock is on. To unlock it, press **Caps Lock** once more.

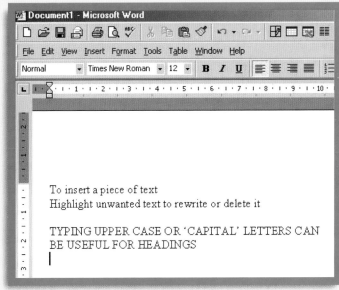

3 To insert words between existing text, move your cursor to the desired position, click and type. Use the **Backspace** key to delete errors to the left of the cursor. You can also delete text by clicking and dragging the mouse pointer over an area of text to highlight it, then pressing the **Backspace** or the **Delete** key. Or, you can highlight the text and type straight over it.

Save your work

Any new document should be saved as soon as possible after creating it, and you should continue to save any changes at regular intervals. This is important because sometimes computers crash, which means that your screen freezes and you have to exit the program without saving your files. So, if you don't save regularly, you run the risk of losing hours of work.

SEE ALSO...

- *Entering text* p 20
- *Import & export files* p 96
- *Create a Web site* p 98

BEFORE YOU START
To save a document for the first time, click on **File** in the Menu bar and choose **Save.** Alternatively, you can click the **Save** button on the toolbar, or use the keyboard shortcut **Ctrl + S**.

1 The first time you save a document, the 'Save As' dialogue box opens. You will need to name your document and choose where to save it. A suggested name, usually the first line, is highlighted in the 'File name' panel. Type a name over it.

Word prompts you to save in the 'My Documents' folder. Click the arrow to the right of the panel if you want to choose a different location.

2 'My Documents' is a good place to store your work. However, it also makes sense, to organise your files into subfolders – for instance, one folder for all your bank letters, another for your Web site, or a folder for each family member. If you want a new folder, click the **Create New Folder** icon and type in a name. To select and open the folder you wish to save into, double-click on it.

Expert advice
To save another version of a document go to the **File** menu and select **Save As**. You can then give the version a new name or choose to store it in an alternative location. This offers a quick and easy method for creating a backup file on floppy, Zip or Jaz disks, or for saving different versions of a file.

Bright idea
Create a template so you don't have to restyle your letters each time. Set up a page the way you want and save it. In the 'Save as type' panel, select Document Template. Next time you create a new document, you can choose your template from the 'New' dialogue box.

4 When you are happy with your options, click the **Save** button. The file name in the blue Title bar at the top of the window changes from 'New document' to the name you have given it. As you work, you need to keep saving your changes. The quickest way is to click the 'floppy disk' icon on your toolbar, or press **Ctrl + S**.

3 Choose how to save your file in the 'Save as type' panel. Most of the time you will save as a 'Word Document'. If you're creating a Web site, save your file as a 'Web Page'. 'Rich Text Format' retains your document setup, but can be opened by many other programs. 'Text Only' saves files as plain text with no styling or formatting, but the text can then be read in almost any program.

Print your work

You are now ready to print out your pages. For the best results, take time to consider the appropriate layout for your document and to view how it will look before printing. Most printers allow you to vary the size of paper you use and to print envelopes and sticky labels. Depending on your printer, you may even be able to produce high quality photographic prints.

SEE ALSO...
- *Format documents p 34*
- *Headers and footers p 52*
- *Address labels p 86*

BEFORE YOU START
Open the Word document you wish to print out. Go to the **File** menu and select **Page Setup**. In the dialogue box, select the **Margins** tab. You can see how your page looks in the 'Preview' section.

1 The margins are set to default measurements which you can increase or decrease. To select a new figure, click the up or down arrows beside each panel.

Alternatively, highlight the existing measurements and type in a new number. You can also change the position of the headers and footers in the 'From edge' section.

2 Select the **Paper Size** tab. Check that the paper size is set to 'A4 210 x 297mm'. If it isn't, or you want a different paper size, click the down arrow and scroll down to choose the correct paper size. Under 'Orientation', select the **Portrait** radio button (vertical) or **Landscape** (horizontal). See the difference between these two options in the 'Preview' section on the right.

Key word
*A radio button **is a small circle beside an option in a dialogue box. To activate the option,** click on the radio button and a dot appears in the circle. To deactivate the option, click on it again, and the dot is removed.*

Look before you print

Before you print anything, it's a good idea to see what your document will look like. Go to the **File** menu and select **Print Preview**, or use the **Print Preview** button on the toolbar. The document is reduced so that the whole page fits the screen, enabling you to check that the layout is correct. To view several pages, select the **Multiple Pages** button on the Preview toolbar and drag across the number of pages you want. To enlarge the view, click on the page itself, or click on the down arrow beside the 'Zoom' button and choose a higher percentage.

4 Go to the **File** menu and click **Print**. Select your printer in the 'Name' panel. Under 'Page range', you can choose to print the whole document ('All'), the 'Current page', or a range of pages ('Pages'). To print a range, you will need to enter the page numbers. If you highlight an area of text in your document, you can click the 'Selection' button to print just that section.

3 Finally, click on the **Layout** tab. Under 'Vertical alignment' you can choose how your text is positioned between the top and bottom margins of the page. Text is automatically aligned to the top of the page, but you can align it to the centre of the page, or the bottom, if you prefer. You can also number your lines and create borders for sections of text or whole pages. Click **OK**.

Bright idea
Printer ink cartridges are expensive. It can work out cheaper to photocopy rather than print multiple colour copies of your document.

6 For double-sided printing, scroll down the options in the 'Print' panel and select **Odd pages**. Pages 1, 3, 5 and so on will then print. Once these are done, turn the printed sheets over, place them in your printer again and select **Even pages** in the 'Print' dialogue box. Click **OK** to print pages 2, 4, 6 and so on.

5 To print more than one copy of a document, click on the up arrow in the 'Number of copies' panel, or highlight the figure and type in the number of copies you want. Select the **Collate** option if you want your copies printed in page order within each set.

Styling Your Text

Choose and size a font

The appearance of any document can be changed dramatically through the use of different fonts, or 'typefaces', and by making text, such as headings a different size. With a manual typewriter, you are limited to the keys on the machine. But with Word, you can use all sorts of different fonts and sizes, even on the same page.

SEE ALSO...
- *Style your text p 30*
- *Format documents p 34*

BEFORE YOU START
To change text to a different font, highlight the text that you want to change. You can then choose to make individual changes quickly, or to make several changes at once.

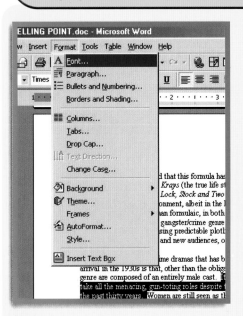

1 When you want to make several changes to your text – to alter font, size and style all at once, for example – it is quicker to do everything at once using the 'Font' dialogue box. Click on the **Format** menu and then on **Font** to open the dialogue box.

2 The default font for the template you are using is highlighted in the 'Font' panel. A line of your own text is shown in this default font in the 'Preview' pane at the bottom.

To see the text in a different font, scroll down the list in the 'Font' panel. Select a font name and look again in the 'Preview' pane to see your text displayed in the selected font.

3 Scroll through, select and view different typefaces (some of them have symbols, not letters). When you have chosen, click **OK** to confirm it. To change the default font for a template you are using, select a font and click on the **Default** button, then on **OK**. This changes the document and the template.

Serif **or** sans-serif

Two common fonts in use today are 'Times New Roman' and 'Arial'. 'Times New Roman' was developed as a typeface for *The Times* newspaper and is a serif font. This means that there are short, fine lines at the ends of the strokes of each character – this was thought to lead the eye smoothly from one letter to the next. 'Arial' was developed later, and is a sans-serif (without serif) font. Research has shown that a serif font is generally more readable when used in long documents, but that a sans-serif font is clearer for anyone who is partially sighted.

> Times New Roman
> Arial

Key word
The height of a font is measured in points, and there are precisely 72 points to an inch. A standard 12-point font measures one-sixth of an inch in height on the page.

5 You can make individual changes to text more quickly by using the 'Formatting' toolbar. To alter the font, highlight your text and click on the down arrow to the right of the 'Font' panel. A drop-down list gives all the fonts available, with their names displayed in the associated typeface.

4 Using the arrows, scroll and select a font size from the list. If the size you want is not there, click on the box, type a figure, press **Return** and your text will change.

The largest standard font size is 72 points. If you need a bigger size, try using WordArt (see page 80). There are also various text effects to choose from, including shadows and embossed type.

6 For quick changes to the size of an item of text, highlight it, then click on the down arrow to the right of the 'Font Size' box on the 'Formatting' toolbar. A drop-down menu lists point sizes. Click on one to select it.

Using columns and bullets

One very effective way of changing the appearance of your document is to put your text in columns. Try this with documents such as newsletters as it makes large amounts of text much easier to read. Alternatively, adding bullet points will help to display lists in a more accessible and logical way, while improving the overall look of your document.

SEE ALSO...
- Format documents p 34
- Using tabs p 40
- Using tables p 48

BEFORE YOU START
Although you can format text into columns after you have finished typing, it is sensible to set the number of columns first, so you have a rough idea of how your pages will look.

1 In the **Format** menu, click on **Columns**. In the dialogue box, select the number of columns you require, either by choosing one of the pre-set options or by typing the number into the appropriate panel. Then, either tick the 'Equal column width' box for evenly spaced columns, or specify the width of each column individually.

2 Your column format will apply to the whole of the document, unless you specify otherwise. If, for example, you need a heading, enter this first, leave a few line spaces and then set up your column format. In the dialogue box, make sure you have selected **This point forward** in the 'Apply to' panel.

The final formatting option allows you to put a visible line between your columns. Click **OK** when your formatting is complete.

3 The cursor appears in your first column for you to begin typing. When the first column is full, your text will run straight into the next one. To force text over into the next column, position your cursor where you want the break, go to the **Insert** menu, select **Break**, and then click **Column break**.

Use your ruler

Column width can be altered quickly using the ruler at the top of the page. Grey areas relate to margins between the columns. Click the edge of a column and drag it to the required size. If you select equal column width, all columns will alter to match. You can change page margins in the same way.

Bright idea
Use the 'Columns' button on the 'Formatting' toolbar as a quick-click method of putting the text in your document into columns.

1 To give your text added emphasis, use bullet points. In the **Format** menu, click on **Bullets and Numbering**. The dialogue box that appears gives you a range of bullet point styles or numbers to choose from. Click on the appropriate tab and select your a style of bullet. Click **OK**. Each time you press 'Return' in your text, a new bullet or number will be added.

4 Your text can then be styled and formatted in the normal way. To avoid awkward line ends in narrow columns, it is a good idea to justify your text. This will give it a more professional look. Highlight the text and click on the **Justify** icon on the 'Formatting' toolbar.

2 From the 'Bullets and Numbering' dialogue box you can also alter the appearance of your bullets. Click on **Customize** then **Font** to alter the size and font. Click on **Bullet** to view a whole range of character options. Select a character, then click **OK**. The 'Bullet position' and 'Text position' sections let you determine how far to indent your bullets, numbers or text. Check the 'Preview' pane for the result.

Using tabs

The 'Tab' feature allows you to align your text – or 'tabulate' it. This is a quick way of moving words across the page, rather than pressing the spacebar repeatedly. While you would create a table to organise lots of information into columns and rows, tabs are a handy way of tidying up a letter, an invoice, or a few simple columns of information.

SEE ALSO...
- *Using columns p 38*
- *Using tables p 48*
- *Sort a list p 92*

BEFORE YOU START
When you are working with tabs, it is a good idea to have the tabs showing. Click on the Show/Hide button in the toolbar to reveal them, if they are not already visible.

1 Microsoft Word opens with tabs set at the default position of 0.5 inches. Pressing the **Tab** key on your keyboard causes the cursor to jump along the line to these preset positions.

2 If you need to set your own tabs instead of using the default ones, highlight the document or the section to which tabs should apply. Go to the **Format** menu and click **Tabs**.

Enter the position of your first tab in the 'Tab stop position' panel, using the ruler at the top of the page as a guide. Add as many tabs as you need, clicking **Set** after each one.

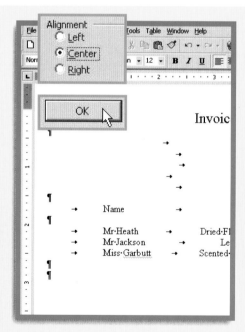

3 The 'Tabs' dialogue box gives you further options, including changing the alignment of your tabs. The default setting is aligned to the left, but you can align the tabs to the middle ('Center') of the text or to the right.

Tab shortcut

A quick way to set your tabs is by using the ruler at the top of the page. Highlight your text. Then, simply by clicking on the ruler at the required tab position, a left-aligned tab will be set. To change the alignment, click on the top left-hand corner to change the icon from left- to centre- or right-aligned tabs.

Bright idea

If you prefer to work in inches go to the Tools *menu and select* Options. **Select the** General **tab and look under 'Measurement units' for a drop-down menu that offers you a choice of units. Select Inches then click** OK.

5 A further option allows you to fill in the space between your tabs with a type of line called a leader. The default setting is 'none', but you can click on the appropriate radio button beneath **Leader** to select dots, a broken line or a solid line. These options work especially well when you are displaying columns of figures.

→ Dried·Flowers	→	£5.99¶
→ Letter·Rack	→	£6.50¶
→ Scented·Drawer·Liners	→	£12.80¶
→ Greetings·Cards	→	£8.25¶
→ Kraft·Paper	→	£2.50¶
→ Ribbon	→	£1.99¶
→ Pen·Holder	→	£15.99¶
→ Picnic·Hamper	→	£110.95¶

Dried Flowers	£5.99
Letter Rack	£6.50
Scented Drawer Liners	£12.80
Greetings Cards	£8.25
Kraft Paper	£2.50
Ribbon	£1.99
Pen Holder	£15.99
Picnic Hamper	£110.95

Dried Flowers	£5.99
Letter Rack	£6.50
Scented Drawer Liners	£12.80
Greetings Cards	£8.25
Kraft Paper	£2.50
Ribbon	£1.99
Pen Holder	£15.99
Picnic Hamper	£110.95

4 If your tabulated text includes figures, select the **Decimal** alignment button. This aligns all your numbers at the decimal point. Selecting **Bar** gives you a vertical dividing line at the position of the tab.

6 The bottom of the Tabs dialogue box has a number of buttons. To delete a tab you've set, select it and click **Clear**. Click **Clear All** to automatically remove all of your tabs.
When you're happy with your settings, click **OK** to return to your document.

Design a letterhead

Using a personalised letterhead will add a touch of flair and individuality to all your correspondence. Once you've created one letterhead, you can follow the same principles to design letterheads for different circumstances – one for business stationery, perhaps. Save your letterhead as a template and you can use it whenever you write a letter.

SEE ALSO...
- *Choose a font p 28*
- *Format documents p 34*
- *Headers and footers p 52*

BEFORE YOU START
Open up a new document, go to the File menu and click on Page Setup.

Click on the Margin tab, set the margins and in the 'From edge' section, set the Header figure. Click OK.

1 A good way to create your letterhead is within the 'Header' section of your document. Go to the **View** menu and click on **Header and Footer**. The cursor automatically appears in the 'Header' section. Type in your name, address and telephone number.

2 Highlight your name, go to the **Format** menu and click on the **Font** tab. Scroll through the list of Fonts and select one. Choose a style and size, clicking on any to view them in the Preview window. Click **OK**. Now style your address in the same way.

Header
Susannah Matthews
104 Chamberlain Avenue
Maidstone, Kent ME16 4LR
Telephone: 01622 442 7272

Key word
The terms *header* **and** *footer*
describe the information that
appears at the top (header)
and bottom (footer) of each page of a
document – for example, running titles,
reference details and page numbers.

Line spacing
The 'Format/Paragraph' dialogue box
allows you to adjust line spacing
between larger sections of highlighted
text. Click on the arrow beside the
'Line spacing' panel, then click on a
suitable measurement. Click **OK**.

4 You can adjust the
spacing above or below
your lines. Select some
or all of your header text and
go to **Format** then
Paragraph. In the 'Spacing'
section, click on the arrows
beside 'Before' or 'After' to
adjust the increment.
Check the 'Preview' panel
to see what your changes
will look like. Click **OK**.

Susannah Matthews
104 Chamberlain Avenue
Maidstone, Kent ME16 4LR
Telephone: 01622 944 8459

3 To position your
letterhead in the centre
of the page, highlight all
of the text in your Header
section, go to the **Format**
menu and choose **Paragraph**.
Click on the black arrow next
to the 'Alignment' panel (right),
and select **Centered** from the
drop-down menu. Click **OK**.

Use your toolbar

The toolbar buttons at the top of the screen help you to style your text quickly. Highlight the text. Click on the relevant button to make it bold, to italicise it or to underline it. Change the position of your text, too, by clicking on the 'Left', 'Centre', 'Right' or 'Justify' alignment buttons.

Bright idea
Save time and effort by using Word's automatic dating facility for your letters. Click where you want the date to appear in your document, go to the **Insert** menu and select **Date and Time**. In the dialogue box choose your preferred style and click **Insert**.

5 When you are happy with your design, save it as a template so that you can use it repeatedly. Go to the **File** menu and select **Save As**. Scroll through the 'Save as type' drop-down menu at the bottom of the dialogue box and select **Document Template**.

6 In the 'Save As' dialogue box you will see from the 'Save in' panel that Word, by default, suggests saving your document in its 'Templates' folder. Type in a suitable name for your template in the 'File name' panel, and then click on the **Save** button.

Let the Wizard help

Microsoft Word has a series of useful wizards that can help you create personalised letterheads. With Word open, go to the **File** menu and click **New**. From the open dialogue box select the **Letters & Faxes** tab and choose the style of letter you would like to use.

The wizard will guide you through the process. You can then save your completed document as a template for future use.

Expert advice

To make changes to your template, go to the **File** menu and select **Open**. From the 'Files of type' panel select **Document Templates**. Double-click on your template in the 'Templates' folder. When your letterhead opens, your name and address will appear as grey text; double-click on it to activate the header. You can now make any necessary changes, then save it.

7 Whenever you want to use your template to write a letter, simply open Word, go to the **File** menu and click on **New**.

Your template will appear under the 'General' tab. Double-click on the icon for your letterhead to open up the template.

8 When the template opens, go to the **File** menu and click **Save As**. Select a folder in which to save your letter, type in a name for it, then click on **Save**. The cursor will flash below your letterhead. Press the **Return** key about five times, then start typing.

AutoFormat your text

The AutoFormat feature applies standard headings and text styles to your documents, giving them a professional finish. You can choose exactly how to format your text and then either have your work formatted automatically as you type, or format a whole document when you have completed it. Word enables you to review and accept or reject the changes.

SEE ALSO...
- *Format documents* *p 34*
- *Wizards & templates* *p 50*
- *AutoCorrect* *p 62*

CHOOSE YOUR STYLE

Whether you are typing a letter, an e-mail or a fax, Word can style your page for you.

Formatting text as you type

To format your text automatically as you type, you need to tell Word what you want it to change. Go to the **Tools** menu and choose **AutoCorrect**. Select the **AutoFormat As You Type** tab and select the options you require. If you want to wait until you have finished before using AutoFormat, untick all of these boxes.

Formatting an existing document

When you have finished typing and are ready to format your document, go to the **Format** menu and select **AutoFormat**.

If you want Word to do this without input from you, select **AutoFormat now**. Otherwise, click **AutoFormat and review each change** so that you can approve changes. Unless instructed, Word formats text as a general document. If you want a letter or an e-mail format, click on the drop-down menu beneath 'Please select a document type...' and choose from the list.

Click on **Options** for preferred settings, which are mostly the same as those on the 'AutoFormat As You Type' tab. However, a few options at the top and bottom of the dialogue boxes differ.

Close up
If you're AutoFormatting a list as you type it, you'll need to tell Word when you've finished the list. To do this, either press the Return key twice, or press it once and then press the Backspace key once.

Close up
For more information on the various AutoFormat options, right-click on an option then left-click on What's This? in the pop-up menu.

Some of your AutoFormat options

Headings Select this option when Word formats a completed document, but leave it unticked when Word formats as you type as it is easier to apply heading styles when you have an overview of the whole document.

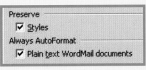

Lists Tick this box if you want to apply the standard style for bulleted and numbered lists. Word removes any bullets or numbers that you've inserted and replaces them with preset styles. Select the **Styles** box in the 'Preserve' section to retain any styles you previously applied to your document, when you run AutoFormat. This option is only available

for styling completed documents. Choose your options, then click **OK** and **OK** again. After a few seconds, your page is reformatted, and the AutoFormat dialogue box appears.

Reviewing changes

If you like the way the document looks, click **Accept All**. If you don't like it, click **Reject All**.

Alternatively, you can go through the entire document, accepting and rejecting each formatting change. Click **Review Changes**. Your text reappears with blue and red 'invisibles', indicating formatting changes that have been made. An explanation of each change is given in the dialogue box.

Accepting or rejecting changes

If you're happy with a formatting change, click the ⇨ **Find** button to accept it and jump to the next change. If you don't like a change, click the **Reject** button to undo it. If you reject a change and then decide to keep it after all, click the **Undo** button on the 'Formatting' toolbar.

To see what the document looks like without the distracting revision marks, select the **Hide Marks** button. When you've finished reviewing the changes, click **Cancel**. To apply the formats you've accepted, click the **Accept All** button in the 'AutoFormat' dialogue box.

Choosing a different look

If you want to change the appearance of your document completely, go to the **Format** menu and select **AutoFormat**. Make sure the **Auto Format and review each change** button is selected and click **OK**. Now click the **Style Gallery** button (see left).

All the document templates are displayed in

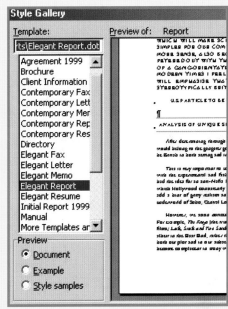

the left pane. Click on a template and preview your document in the pane on the right.

Alternatively, select **Example** in the 'Preview' section, to preview a sample document.

Click the **OK** button when you have found a template that suits your needs.

Bright idea
If you are unhappy with the way that AutoFormat has changed your pages, press the Undo *button on the 'Formatting' toolbar or choose* Undo *from the* Edit *menu.*

Key word
Invisibles **are the symbols used to represent specific instances of formatting in a document, such as a paragraph break, indent or tab. They are only for visual reference on screen, and do not print with the rest of your document.**

Using tables

Tables provide an ideal structure for organising and presenting information. Table data can be sorted alphabetically, numerically, or by date, and you can treat the table like a mini-spreadsheet and use it to perform calculations. Word 2000 also lets you move the table around the page, or position it exactly where you want within text.

SEE ALSO...
● *Using columns p 38*
● *Using tabs p 40*
● *Wizards & templates p 50*

BEFORE YOU START
Think about how many columns and rows you are likely to need – a rough sketch might help you to decide. Extra rows are easy to add, but new columns require a little more sorting out.

1 In the **Table** menu, click on **Insert Table** and select the required number of columns and rows in the dialogue box. 'Fixed column width' spreads columns out evenly across the page. 'AutoFit to contents' widens columns to fit typed text or graphics, while 'AutoFit to window' allows the table to fit a Web browser window.

2 Click the **Autoformat** button to choose one of the preset 'Table AutoFormat' options. The list on the left-hand side of the dialogue box gives you a number of choices, together with a preview on the right-hand side.
Further formatting choices can be made by ticking or unticking the boxes provided. Check the preview pane to see what effect your choices have, then click **OK** to confirm your choices. Click **OK**.

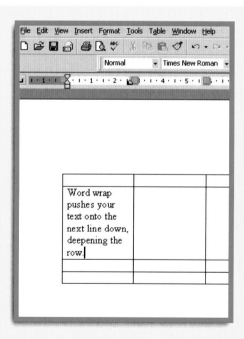

3 Type in your text. To move from cell to cell, press the **Tab** key, or use your mouse to position your cursor. You can type any amount of text in a cell, as the size of all the cells in that row will increase to accommodate it.

Formatting your table

To customise your table, select **Table Properties** from the **Table** menu. From here, you can alter the position of your table on the page and the way text wraps around it. Clicking on the **Borders and Shading** button allows you to alter the appearance of each cell and to show or hide as much of the grid as needed.

Watch out

When you draw a table, you need to choose the style, colour and line width before you begin to draw. It can be quicker to insert a table and adjust the formatting later.

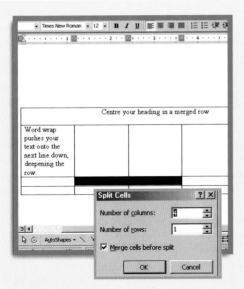

5 For a more complex, customised table, click on the **Table** menu and choose **Draw Table**. Your cursor changes to a pencil shape and the 'Tables and Borders' toolbar appears. You can use this toolbar to change the line width, colour and style of your table. To draw a red table for example, click on the **Pencil** button and select red in the drop-down menu.

4 To merge cells together – so you can type a heading, for example – click and drag your mouse over the cells to select them. Go to the **Table** menu and select **Merge Cells**. To split cells, to create more than originally specified, highlight the row, click the **Table** menu, select **Split Cells** and change the number of columns. Click **OK**.

6 Create the outline of the table by clicking on the page and dragging the pencil diagonally until the table is the size you want. Draw in the row and column lines by dragging the pencil cursor from one edge of the box to the other. Then close the toolbar to enter your text.

Wizards and templates

Every time you create a new document, you are offered the 'Blank Document' template, which is an empty document with a pre-defined layout. However, there are a variety of other templates available, some of which are also wizards. These lead you step by step through common procedures, such as creating your curriculum vitae or a fax.

SEE ALSO...
- *Design a letterhead p 42*
- *Make address labels p 86*
- *Create a Web site p 98*

BEFORE YOU START
*Click on the **File** menu and select **New** to open the 'New' dialogue box. This has nine template and wizard tab headings, with items from calendars and brochures to Web pages and faxes.*

1 To use a letter template, click on the **Letters & Faxes** tab. Select one of the three letter styles – 'Elegant', 'Professional' or 'Contemporary'. View the style in the 'Preview' pane on the right. Select one you want, and click **OK**.

2 The template tells you where to enter your details. To replace this text, just highlight it and type in your details – for example, highlight the heading 'Company Name Here', then type in your own company name. Where instructions are given in square brackets, just click inside them to highlight the words and then type in your own text.

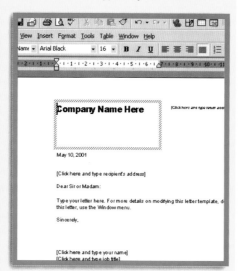

1 To use a wizard to make a CV, or résumé, for example, click on the **Other Documents** tab, select **Résumé Wizard** and click **OK**. On the left is a list of the various stages. Green indicates where you are. Click **Next**.

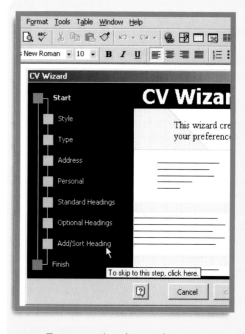

That's amazing!
You can create your own templates to re-use as often as you wish. To save a document as a template, click on **File**, then **Save As**. Name your file. In the 'Save as type' panel, select **Document Template**. Your new template will be added to the other templates available when you create a new document.

Watch out
Many of the templates provided by Word were created specifically for American users. This means that they may not always be appropriate in the UK.

3 Select the personal items you would like in your CV from a list of options. The next, window offers standard options for section headings while the following one has specialised options. Click **Next**. You can also type any heading that has not so far been on offer, and edit those already selected.

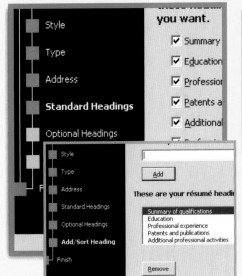

2 Select which style you want by clicking the appropriate radio button. Click **Next**. You will then be asked about the type of CV you want to create. Choose from the options then click **Next**. Click in the relevant boxes in the following window, typing in your name and other details. Click **Next**.

4 When you reach the end of the wizard, click on the **Finish** button. Your customised document template opens with your selected headings, ready to receive your details. You can now start to type them in.

Headers and footers

Headers and footers enable you to add running information to your pages, such as page numbers. They appear in the top or bottom margins of your document, outside the normal print area. Anything that you insert in a header or footer appears on every page of your document, unless you specify otherwise.

BEFORE YOU START
To add a header or footer to a document, click on the **View** menu and choose **Header and Footer**. A toolbar appears that allows you to enter text and style it as you wish.

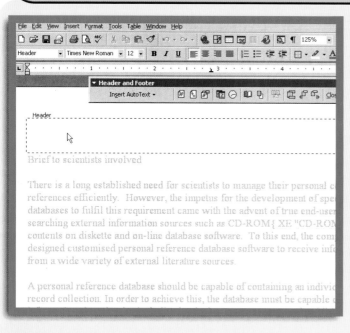

1 Once you have the 'Header and Footer' toolbar on screen, you will notice that your cursor is flashing on the left of the header, ready for you to enter text, or even a image. You will also notice that the text in the main body of your document looks faint, meaning that it is not accessible or editable while you are in this view.

2 You can align your header text to the left, centre or right using the toolbar buttons (below). Press the **Tab** key to move along the box and type in your header text. To move from the header to the footer, click on the **Switch Between Header and Footer** button on the toolbar. Type your text into the footer as appropriate.

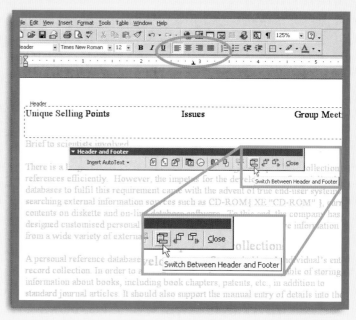

Using the toolbar

You'll find lots of useful features in the 'Header and Footer' toolbar: Use 'Insert Date' and 'Insert Time' to show when you created a document. Use 'Page Setup' to set your options, such as having different headers and footers on odd and even pages.

Use 'Show Previous' and 'Show Next' to jump between headers or footers. By default, headers and footers are identical on every page. If you want different footers on each page, jump to your next footer and click the **Same as Previous** button to deselect it. Now type your text.

Watch out

If you just type in your page number in a header or footer, this same number will be repeated on every page. Click and use the Insert Page Number *button instead (see Step 3).*

4 You can style the header and footer as you would any text. Click the formatting buttons to increase the font size or to make it bold or italic. You can also add a border. Highlight your header or footer, go to the **Format** menu and choose **Borders and Shading**. Select a line style, then click the appropriate border in the 'Preview' pane. Click **OK**, then **Close** to return to your text.

3 To add a page number, position your cursor where you want it to appear in your footer and click on the **Insert Page Number** icon on the Header and Footer toolbar. Style the page number by clicking on the **Format Page Number** icon. In the dialogue box, select a format from the drop-down menu. Choose what number to start the pages with under 'Page numbering'. Click **OK**.

Thesaurus and Word Count

Sometimes it can be hard to find the right word, or you can find yourself using the same one repeatedly. If you are stuck for inspiration, you can try a thesaurus for an eloquent alternative. A faster solution, however, is to consult Word's own Thesaurus. There is also a word counting facility, which can help you stick to a brief when writing essays or reports.

SEE ALSO...

● *Spelling and grammar* p 58
● *Find and replace* p 64

BEFORE YOU START
*Go to the **Tools** menu, click **Language** and **Set Language**. In the dialogue box, select the language you wish to use. Remember that UK and US English are different.*

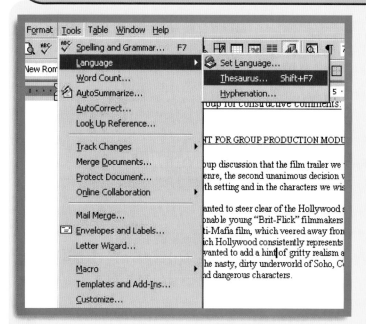

1 Open an existing document that you wish to edit, or type your text. Now highlight the word you wish to look up in the Thesaurus. Go to the **Tools** menu and select **Language**, then **Thesaurus** to open the 'Thesaurus' dialogue box. Or you can use the keyboard shortcut to the Thesaurus, **Shift + F7**.

2 The 'Looked Up' panel displays your chosen word. The 'Meanings' panel lists possible definitions of your word, indicating whether they are verbs (v.) or nouns (n.) and so on. Click on the correct meaning to select it. Opposite is a list of synonyms – words with the same meaning as your word. The Thesaurus' recommended substitute is in the 'Replace with Synonym' panel.

Count your words

For a detailed breakdown of your document, go to the **Tools** menu and select **Word Count**. The Word Count box will display the number of pages, words, characters, paragraphs and lines in your document. Click **Close** to exit.

If you want a breakdown of just part of your document, highlight that section, then go to the **Tools** menu again and select **Word Count**.

That's amazing!

You can use the Thesaurus to look up a word that is not already in your document. Place your cursor on a blank section of the page and open the Thesaurus. Type your word in the 'Insert' panel, and click the **Look Up** button. Your word will appear in the 'Looked Up' panel, with the synonyms and antonyms listed on the right.

4 You can also look up alternatives for any of the synonyms listed in the right-hand panel.

Select a word and click **Look Up**. Your choice will now appear in the 'Looked Up' panel, with a list of synonyms on the right.

To return to your original word, click **Previous** – or click the arrow on the 'Looked Up' panel and select your word from the drop-down menu.

3 If you want to use the suggested replacement, click **Replace**.

If you want to use a different word, scroll down the list of synonyms and double-click your preferred choice. Note that a word listed with '(Antonym)' after it has the opposite meaning to your word. If you want to exit the Thesaurus, click **Cancel**.

AutoCorrect your text

Word's AutoCorrect feature detects and corrects common spelling mistakes, grammatical errors and incorrect use of capital letters. Furthermore, if you know that you often make specific typographical errors, such as typing "seperate" instead of "separate", you can add them to a list – AutoCorrect will then rectify the mistakes for you automatically as you type.

SEE ALSO...

● *AutoFormat p 46*
● *Spelling and grammar p 58*

MAXIMUM EFFICIENCY

To make the most of the AutoCorrect feature, you should set it up to suit your own work requirements.

Go to the **Tools** menu and choose **AutoCorrect**. Select the **AutoCorrect** tab. The first four boxes relate to ways in which AutoCorrect can help

with capitalisation. The most useful options are 'Capitalize first letter of sentences' and 'Capitalize names of days'. Click on a box to select it.

It is a good idea to set up exceptions to the rule. To do this, click on the **Exceptions** button

and select the **First Letter** tab. There is a list of abbreviations in the 'Don't capitalize after' panel. To add to it, click in the top panel and type in any word commonly followed by a full stop – for example, the abbreviation 'ie'. Click **Add**. To get rid of an item, select it and click **Delete**.

The 'INitial CAps' tab allows you to make exceptions to the autocorrection of two capital letters at the beginning of a word. The third tab, 'Other Corrections', is for any words that AutoCorrect might detect as misspelt, but which

you do not wish to be changed. Click **OK** to return to the AutoCorrect dialogue box.

Correcting common misspellings

In the AutoCorrect dialogue box under the 'Autocorrect' tab, click in the box next to 'Replace text as you type' if it isn't already selected, then look at the list of possible substitutions in the panel below.

The first few entries are keyboard formulas that you can enter to get certain symbols – for

instance, if you type **(c)**, Word will replace it with ©. Scroll down the list to see a number of common misspellings and typing errors that will be corrected

---

Watch out
When you enter words you commonly mistype in the 'Replace' panel, remember to make sure that they are not actual words – that is, those you might find in the dictionary. If they are, you may find some of your text has been corrected in error after you run AutoCorrect.

Bright idea
If you often use other styles of typed letters, such as superscript for fractions and dates, typing them into the AutoCorrect box saves having to select your text and change style manually.

for you automatically if you use this option. You can even edit words in this list.

Select a word, click in the 'Replace' or 'With' panel, and type in your amendment. Then click on the **Replace** button. You can also **Delete** any spellings that are irrelevant to your work.

To add your own words, type your misspelling in the empty 'Replace' panel, and type the

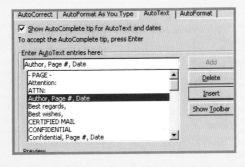

correction in the empty 'With' panel. Click **Add** to add it to the list.

If you select 'Automatically use suggestions from the spelling checker', AutoCorrect will use corrections offered by the dictionary. Be aware that you might not always agree with the dictionary's substitutions, so it is a good idea to check any changes made as you type.

AUTOTEXT
Use this feature to save time when typing dates, letter openers and closers, and other phrases you regularly use.

Select the **AutoText** tab and click the box next to 'Show AutoComplete tip for AutoText and dates'.

When appropriate, a 'ScreenTip' pops up as you type, offering to fill in relevant text – such as today's date. Scroll down the 'Enter AutoText entries here' menu to view a selection of

frequently used words or phrases. To add your own word or phrase to the list, type into the blank panel under 'Enter AutoText entries here' and then click **Add**.

Add a paragraph to AutoText
It is a good idea to add sentences or paragraphs you use often, such as your address, to AutoText. In your document, type some text you often use. Highlight it, go to the **Insert** menu and click **AutoText**, then **New**, to open the 'Create AutoText' dialogue box. The first couple of words are selected as the AutoText name, but you can

change this. Click **OK**.

If you selected the 'Show AutoComplete tip for AutoText and dates' box, simply type the first few letters of the phrase or name of your AutoText entry. A ScreenTip will appear showing your text. To accept the entry, press **Return**. If you did not select the 'Show AutoComplete for AutoText and dates' tip box, go to the **Insert** menu, select **AutoText**, then the name of your entry. It will appear on the page.

Put AutoText on your toolbar
For easy access, you can add the 'AutoText' button to your toolbar. Go to the **Insert** menu and select **Autotext**, then **AutoText** again. Click the **Show Toolbar** button.

Click the **AutoText** toolbar button to open the 'AutoCorrect' dialogue box. Click on **All Entries** to view and select entries. To add a new entry, highlight your phrase and click **New** to open the 'Create AutoText' dialogue box. Click **OK** to save.

AutoSummarize
AutoSummarize scans your document and picks out the key points. It's useful for providing a summary of reports or any other kind of structured article.

Click the **Tools** menu and select **AutoSummarize**. You're given four summary options: highlighting key points; creating a new document containing the summary; inserting the summary at the top of the existing document; or hiding everything except the summary. Click the option you wish to view. Click **OK**.

Bright idea
If you accept the first few words of your text as a name when creating an AutoText entry, when you start to type those words, the ScreenTip will automatically pop up.

Change your preferences

Word comes with predefined settings suitable for general word processing use. However, you can change these settings if you feel that others would be more useful. For example, if the ruler at the top of the screen measures in inches, but you prefer to work in centimetres, it is a simple matter of changing the measurement setting to your choice.

SEE ALSO...
- *Spelling and grammar* p 58
- *AutoCorrect* p 62
- *Edit a toolbar* p 68

YOUR CHOICE

In the Tools menu, click Options. Here, you can customise common tasks, such as editing, saving and printing your work, so that they are carried out automatically in the way you prefer.

Viewing options

You will see a dialogue box with two rows of tabs which give you access to preference options.

You will want to change some preferences more than others. Click on the **View** tab. This dialogue box is divided into four sections, and allows you to alter how a page looks on screen. Clicking on any box adds a tick, which means that particular option has been selected.

The uppermost section, 'Show', allows you to select whether to see screen items such as the Status bar, vertical and horizontal scroll bars, screen tips and other page-related options, such as highlights and bookmarks.

'Formatting marks' lets you determine which invisibles are shown, for example, paragraph or tab marks. This is useful for document layout and it is a good idea to tick the **All** box.

'Print and Web Layout options' and 'Outline and Normal options' determine which formatting objects are visible when working on a document.

General options

Use the 'General' tab to change measurement units from inches to centimetres or millimetres, or the typesetting measurements from points to picas. You can also choose how many entries you want to show in the 'Recently used file list' – at the bottom of the 'File' menu – which provides you with a quick way of opening a document that you have recently worked on.

Customising toolbars

To change your toolbar options, click on the **Tools** menu and select **Customize**, then the **Toolbars** tab. Ticking a box next to a toolbar's name means that this toolbar will appear automatically when you launch Word. You can click on as many toolbars as you need.

Clicking on the **Options** tab allows you to change the appearance of your toolbars' drop-down menus and the size of your toolbar icons.

Edit preferences

Editing functions, such as selecting, cutting and pasting text and styling paragraphs, can all be modified in this section.

For instance, if you select the 'Drag-and-drop text editing' box, you can highlight text in your document, then just click and drag it to place it somewhere else. If you select 'Overtype mode', then you can type straight over existing text,

without highlighting it. Click 'Use smart cut and paste' for spaces to be added or removed as necessary when you move text around.

Printing and saving

If you find that you often have to change the setup in 'Print' dialogue boxes, or to save and make backups when working in Word, it may be more efficient to set your printing and saving preferences here.

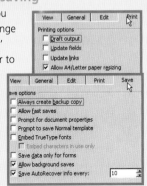

For instance, you can save on ink if you print out all your documents as 'Draft', selecting a higher quality only for letters and other important items.

Spelling and Grammar preferences

You can specify whether you want Word to

indicate spelling or grammar errors as you type. You can also select a UK or US dictionary to check your spelling.

File locations

When you save something, Word anticipates where you will wish to save it. For instance, you might save your documents into the 'My Documents' folder. You can change these locations by clicking the **Modify** button and selecting folders for the different file types.

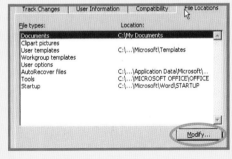

Compatibility preferences

If someone sends you a Word file that is in an older version, click on the drop-down menu under 'Recommended options for' and select the

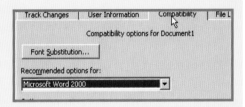

appropriate version. In the 'Options' panel, Word selects the viewing choices it recommends for this document. This affects the way the file appears on screen, but doesn't permanently alter the file.

User information preferences

Each time a document is saved, user information is added to the file properties, such as the name of the person who created that document and their e-mail address. Use this dialogue box to update that information.

Tracking text changes

'Track Changes' allows you to monitor alterations to a document in different ways – for example, by underlining inserted text in red or striking through deleted text in green. This is particularly useful if more than one person is working on the same document, and making lots of changes.

Close up
Using the 'Spelling and Grammar' tab in 'General' options, you can override a previous spelling check in Word and re-check a document – for instance, if you do not want your grammar checked as you work.

Edit a toolbar

Toolbars are the rows of buttons at the edges of your window that you click on to perform commands. If you position your mouse pointer over a button, you can see a description of its function. There are 16 basic toolbars, each devoted to a particular aspect of word processing. You can add buttons to an existing toolbar or create your own toolbar from scratch.

SEE ALSO...
- *Explore the program p 16*
- *WordArt & Autoshape p 80*

BEFORE YOU START
Three toolbars and a ruler normally sit at the top of the Word window.

From the top, you will see the Menu bar, then the Standard toolbar, and finally the Formatting toolbar.

1 To move any toolbar, click its 'Move' handle – the grey bar on the far left – and drag it to a new location. You can move a toolbar to any position on your screen, or swap its position with one of the other toolbars at the top.

2 Click on the small arrow on the far right-hand side of any toolbar and then on **Add or Remove Buttons**. You will see a menu of all the buttons available for that toolbar. On the left of each icon is a small box which is ticked if the button is already selected and present on the toolbar.

3 To add or remove a button from the toolbar, click the relevant item once. A tick will appear if you're adding a button, and disappear if you are removing it.

Click **Reset Toolbar** to return the toolbar to its default settings. When you've finished making changes, click on the window to return to your document.

Bright idea
Clear your work area by closing toolbars you don't need. Drag them onto the document and click on the Close *button. Position others along the edges of your screen, where they automatically snap into place.*

That's amazing!
If you use a set of toolbar commands often, you can save your toolbar settings for use in a template. Go to the 'Customize' dialogue box, click on **Save in** under the 'Commands tab' and choose to save with whichever template you want.

5 Select the **Commands** tab. Here you can further customise toolbars by adding more specialised buttons. Under 'Categories' is a list of all the different types of commands – 'File' menu commands, fonts and so on. Select a category, then scroll through the 'Commands' list in the pane on the right to see what is available.

To see every single one of Word's functions, select **All Commands**.

4 To display more toolbars on screen, go to the **Tools** menu and select **Customize**. Under the 'Toolbars' tab is a list of all Word's toolbars. The ticked items are already available.

Click any of the items on the list to select or deselect them. Click **Reset** to go back to Word's default settings.

6 To add a command to a toolbar, select the item from the list and drag it onto a toolbar in Word's main window. If you put it in the wrong place, just drag it to a different position.

With the 'Customize' dialogue box open, you can also delete buttons. Just click and then drag and drop the button off the toolbar.

Toolbars for special tasks

Extra toolbars appear automatically when you perform certain functions, such as adding headers and footers, or creating a box with the 'Text Box' tool on the 'Drawing' toolbar. Some of these are displayed only while you are working on the particular feature and disappear when you click on a different part of the document. Others can be added to your current selection of toolbars to make repetitive tasks simpler.

Bright idea
If you find you now have too many toolbars, go back to the Toolbars tab and select only Standard, Formatting *and* Menu bar. **Click on** Reset **and then on** OK **to return the original settings.**

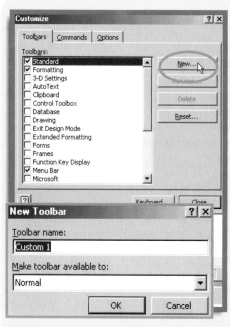

7 To create your very own toolbar, which you can assign to a template or an individual document, select the **Toolbars** tab and click the **New** button. Type an appropriate name in the 'Toolbar name' box and click **OK**.

8 Your toolbar is added to the list, and appears to the left of the 'Customize' dialogue box as a small grey square. Select the **Commands** tab. Choose a Category, then click and drag the buttons you want, one at a time, from the list on the right onto your toolbar. You can edit and change an individual icon by selecting it, clicking on **Modify Selection** and then on the appropriate command.

9 When you have finished, click **Close**. Your toolbar is now displayed on the screen. Click and drag it to the position you want it to occupy. You can select it or deselect it in the same way as the other toolbars.

TOOLBARS GALORE

Make yourself familiar with the toolbars available to find out which will be of use to you. There are some you will probably never use, while others will save you a tremendous amount of time when you want to do certain tasks. Do not be afraid to edit toolbars to make them work for you.

DRAWING

Add all kinds of designs and embellishments to personalise your documents.

Select Object · AutoShapes menu · Arrow · Oval · Insert WordArt · Fill Color · Font Color · Dash Style · Close button · Shadow

'Draw' drop-down menu · Free Rotate · Line · Rectangle · Text Box · Insert ClipArt · Line Color · Line Style · Arrow Style · 3-D

WORDART

Commands to incorporate a host of special typestyles.

WordArt Gallery · WordArt Shape · Text Wrapping · WordArt Vertical Text

Insert WordArt · WordArt Character Spacing

Edit Text · Format WordArt · Free Rotate · WordArt Same Letter Heights · WordArt Alignment

WEB

Facilitates surfing on the Web and stores favourite addresses.

Stop Current jump · Refresh Current page · Start Page · Search the Web · Favorites menu · Go menu · Show Only Web Toolbar

MICROSOFT

Instant access to other Microsoft programs you may have.

PowerPoint · MS Access · MS Project · MS Publisher

Back and Forward · Address

Excel · MS Mail · MS Fox Pro · MS Schedule

Viewing options

There are several different ways of viewing the document on your screen. If you are designing a Web page, making a brochure or writing a letter, you will probably want to see what it will look like when it is printed or published. Having an overview of the document will also make it easier to restructure it. Find out how Word's options can make your work easier on the eyes.

SEE ALSO...
- *Print your work p 24*
- *Create a Web site p 98*

CHOOSING YOUR VIEW

'Normal View' is the default setting for seeing documents on screen but there are several alternatives.

To access the different options for viewing your document, click on the **View** menu and choose the one you want.

Normal

In 'Normal' view, the text fills the space available in the window and the various toolbars are all accessible. Page and section breaks are indicated by a dotted line. However, in 'Normal' View some graphics and layout features do not appear or are not obvious.

Web Layout

This view enables you to see what the features of the Web page you are creating will look like when it is published on the Internet.

To see your layout in the Web browser, click on the **File** menu and select **Web Page Preview**.

Print Layout

This allows you to work on and view your document as it will look when printed. The whole page is displayed, including margins, headers and footers, columns, and pictures you have added.

Outline

This structural overview only shows headings. A new toolbar opens up and you can write, select, edit and style all your headings at once, or individually. To restructure the entire document, click on the symbol to the left of a heading, and drag it to a new position.

Full Screen

This is a 'click on', 'click off' function available in the various views. All menus and toolbars are removed, so your document fills the entire screen.

Zoom

A magnifying lens, lets you enlarge or reduce text in any view. Use 'enlarge' if you find yourself peering at the screen or want to work in detail on an image. Use 'reduce' to view whole pages.

Expert advice

You can quickly enlarge or reduce your view of the screen. Just click on the down arrow on the far right of your 'Formatting' toolbar and select a higher or lower percentage of the document size.

Bright idea

Instead of using the 'View' menu, click the shortcut icons on the bottom left of your screen. Hold the pointer over the button to see what each one does.

Using Graphics

Add a picture

Inserting graphics or pictures into a document can instantly add impact and clarity to your subject. You can either use your own pictures, or choose from the vast gallery of ClipArt provided by Word. Desktop publishing is also made easy by allowing you to integrate illustrations and charts with your text, to produce professional-looking results.

SEE ALSO...
- Create a newsletter p 76
- WordArt & AutoShape p 80
- Add a background p 82

BEFORE YOU START
Open a document. You may already have a picture that you want to insert but don't worry if you haven't – you can easily find graphics stored on your computer or on a CD.

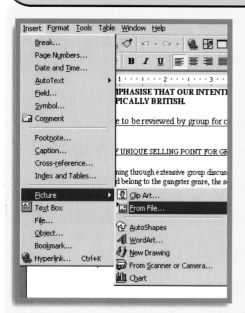

1 To add a graphic to your document, first position the cursor where you would like to insert the image. Next, go to the **Insert** menu and select **Picture**. If you wish to use an image on your PC, a CD-ROM or a floppy disk, select **From File**.

2 The 'Insert Picture' dialogue box appears on screen. It automatically shows the 'My Pictures' folder, where you'll see some sample images. Click the 'Look in' panel's drop-down menu to browse for your image file.

Note that graphics are previewed on the right of the 'Insert Picture' dialogue box. To view a file, click it once. To select it, click **Insert**.

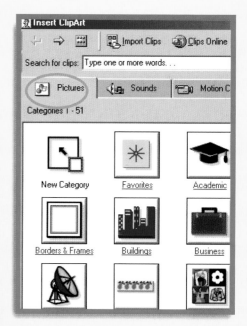

3 Alternatively, to insert a picture from Word's Clip Gallery, go to the **Insert** menu and choose **Picture** then **Clip Art**. Ensure that the 'Pictures' tab is selected, then click on the subject category you wish to browse.

Text-Wrapping
You can wrap the text around the graphic in different ways by right-clicking on the graphic, selecting **Format picture**, then choosing the **Layout tab**. Here you will see a variety of wrapping styles. Select one and click **OK**.

Watch out
Although it is fine to use ClipArt in documents such as newsletters and flyers, it is not legal to use it for promotional or marketing material, nor can you publish a document containing it.

5 Only the most common ClipArt files are installed and available instantly on your computer. Sometimes, when you click on your chosen picture you may be asked to insert your Word CD in order to download that clip. In which case, click the **Cancel button** and insert the CD. Wait until the CD has loaded, then try to insert the picture once again.

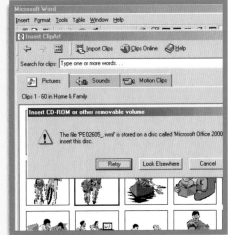

4 If this category does not contain any suitable ClipArt, click the **Back** button at the top left of the dialogue box to return to the main categories. To search for a suitable image, type a relevant word into the 'Search for clips' panel and press **Return**.

6 To insert your chosen ClipArt, click the image and select the **Insert clip** icon. Close the dialogue box to view the graphic in your document. To resize the image, click on it then using a handle (above), click and drag. Use the picture toolbar to adjust brightness, contrast and colours.

Create a family newsletter

One of the best ways to keep family members in touch, no matter how far apart they are, is by compiling a regular newsletter. The first task is to ask your relatives whether they would like to contribute any news, such as a new job or a recently passed exam, favourite recipes, or even poems they have written. The rest takes just a few steps in Word.

SEE ALSO...
- *Using columns* p 38
- *Spelling and grammar* p 58
- *Create a Web site* p 98

BEFORE YOU START
*Open a new A4 document, name it and save it. Go to the **File** menu and click on* *Page Setup. Select the **Margins** tab, then set the sizes for the 'Top', 'Bottom', 'Left' and 'Right' margins. Click **OK**.*

1 Type in your heading, then press the **Return** key. Type in all of your articles, giving each its own title. Press the **Return** key between each article to leave a line space. Once all of your text is typed, you can run a spell check. In the **Tools** menu, click on **Spelling and Grammar** and check for any suspect words.

2 Add a ClipArt image (see page 74). Click on it and go to the **Format** menu and select **Picture**. Click the **Layout** tab, then the **Advanced** button. Select the **Text Wrapping** tab and click on **Tight**. Click the **Picture Position** tab and tick 'Move object with text', so the image is locked to the paragraph of text around it. Click **OK** twice.

Applying settings
To apply your column settings to the area of the document below the heading, click on the arrow to the right of the 'Apply to' panel, scroll through and select **This point forward**.

4 Text is usually easier to read if you set it out in columns. Place the cursor at the start of your first article, go to the **Format** menu and click on **Columns**.

Select **Two** in the 'Presets' section. Set the column width and spacing. To run a vertical line between the columns, ensure the 'Line between' box is ticked, then click **OK**.

3 Highlight your heading and go to the **Format** menu, then click on **Font**. Choose a font, style, size and colour. As this is an informal document, choose a fun font. You can see how it looks in the 'Preview' panel.

For a distinctive effect, you could check the 'Shadow' box and select a dotted rule in the 'Underline style' box.

Adjusting line spacing

To adjust line spacing, highlight the article (not the heading), click on **Format** then **Paragraph**. Under 'Spacing', click on the down arrow in the 'Line spacing' panel, and select an option. If you know which point size you want, click **Exactly** and select the size in the 'At' panel.

To increase the space between paragraphs by a further 1 point at a time, click on the up arrow next to the 'After' panel. Click **OK**.

Close up
To use photographs in your newsletter, scan them in, or get them scanned at a bureau, and save them on your PC. Go to the Insert menu, select Picture then click From File. Find your photograph and click Insert.

5 Highlight the heading of your first article, go to the **Format** menu and select **Font**. Now choose a font, style and size.

If you are printing in colour, click on the arrow to the right of the 'Font color' panel, scroll through and pick a colour. Click **OK**.

6 Now highlight and style the first paragraph of your first article in the same way. Choose a bold font style to make it stand out. Continue to highlight and style the rest of the text and headings using similar fonts, styles and sizes.

Drop Caps

In the 'Drop Cap' dialogue box, click on the **Dropped** icon in the 'Position' section. Select the number of lines you want it to drop by in the 'Lines to drop' panel to adjust its size, and click **OK**.

Expert advice

To make changes to a template in Word, go to the **File** menu and select **Open**. From the 'Files of type' box select **Document Templates**. Double-click on your template in the 'Templates' folder. When your newsletter opens, you can simply type over existing text and headings, and they will retain their style. You can also cut and replace any ClipArt or photos.

8 If you want to produce a regular newsletter, save your document as a template. Go to the **File** menu and select **Save As**. Scroll though file options in the 'Save as type' panel and select **Document Template**. Word will save your newsletter in its 'Templates' folder ready to use for your next edition. Finally, click on **Save**.

7 To add a large capital letter at the start of a paragraph, click your cursor in the paragraph, go to the **Format** menu and select **Drop Cap**. Apply the settings in the dialogue box (see 'Drop Caps', above), and click **OK**.
To preview how your document looks, go to the **File** menu and select **Print Preview**.

Mail Merge

When you need to send the same letter to lots of people, using the mail merge facility is a fantastic time saver. You can create one letter and merge it with a data file of all the relevant names and addresses. You can use this feature for all kinds of mass mailings, whether you're writing to family and friends, club members or business contacts.

SEE ALSO...
- Address labels p 86
- Use macros p 90

BEFORE YOU START
You may wish to use data such as names and addresses from Microsoft Access, but you can also create a new data source while setting up the mail merge (see page 86).

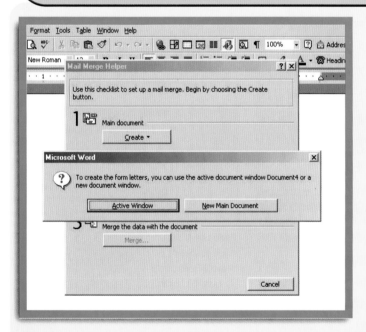

2 Under the 'Data source' heading, click on **Get Data**. If you have a data source, such as a list of names and addresses, choose **Open Data Source**, find the file you want and click **Open**.

Then select the **Edit Main Document** button. If you do not have a data source, click on **Create Data Source**. Follow the instructions in 'Make address labels' (page 86, steps 3 and 4).

1 Open a new document, go to the **Tools** menu and select **Mail Merge**. Under the 'Main document' heading, click the **Create** button and choose **Form Letters**. You are asked if you want to use the 'Active Window' (the document you're in) or to create a 'New Main Document'. Click **Active Window**.

That's amazing!
Use Mail Merge to print addresses directly onto envelopes. In step one, after clicking **Create**, select **Envelopes** instead of 'Form Letters' and follow step two, choosing your envelope size and orientation in the 'Envelope options' dialogue box. Then click **Insert Merge Field** in the Envelope address box and select the fields you want to use.

Close up
You may need to alter some field names. Take time to think about those relevant to your own data, removing any you do not want, typing over and adding others and leave an extra one, which you can edit later.

Bright idea
Always check your work before you print, by choosing Merge to New Document. If you select Merge to Printer, all the letters will be printed in one go and you will not have the opportunity to check them.

4 Once you are happy with the form letter, click the **Merge to New Document** button on the Mail Merge toolbar. Data is rapidly inserted into a series of form letters, with one letter per record. These will appear on the screen, ready for you to check. To print your letters, go to the **File** menu and select **Print**.

3 Now start to type your form letter. Using the Return and Spacebar keys, click where you wish to insert a merge field. Go to the **Insert Merge Field** menu on the Mail Merge toolbar at the top of the screen and select the field name (see 'Close up' above). Word inserts a dividing space between fields for you. Use 'Return' to position the fields.

Make address labels

Addressing numerous envelopes is a repetitive and time-consuming task. However, Word's label printing feature can save you a lot of effort and makes your envelopes look professional. If you already have address lists stored on your PC, you can use the merge feature to print the details as labels, or create sheets of address labels for individual contacts.

SEE ALSO...
● *Wizards & templates p 50*
● *Mail merge p 84*

BEFORE YOU START
Open a blank Word document, name it and save it. You may have an address list already, but don't worry if you haven't – we'll show you how to do this with the 'Mail Merge Helper'.

1 Go to the **Tools** menu and select **Mail Merge**. The 'Mail Merge Helper' wizard will appear on screen to guide you through the process. Now click on the **Create** button, and select **Mailing Labels**.
   A dialogue box will ask you which document you want to use for your mailing list. Click **Active Window**.

2 Under step 2 of the 'Mail Merge Helper' dialogue box, click **Get Data**. If you have an address list ready and waiting, choose **Open Data Source** from the drop-down menu, and locate and select your list. Now go to Step 5 of this feature.
   If you don't have an address list, select **Create Data Source** and go to Step 3.

Key word
A field marks a place in your document. When you perform a merge, the fields instruct your program where to put the information you're merging into your document, such as names and addresses.

Close up
Sheets of address labels come in various sizes. Each page size and configuration of labels has its own reference number. For A4 printers, one of the most popular is the L7163, with 14 labels on an A4 sheet.

Create Data Source

A mail merge data source is composed of rows of data. The first ro
header row. Each of the columns in the header row begins with a f

Word provides commonly used field names in the list below. You ca
field names to customize the header row.

Field name:

Field names in header row:

Title
FirstName
LastName
JobTitle
Company
Address1
Address2

Add Field Name ➤➤

Remove Field Name

MS Query...

OK

4 The wizard recognises that your list doesn't contain any data yet. Click **Edit Data Source**. In the 'Data Form' dialogue box, enter your addresses. Click **OK** when you've finished. Now go to the **Tools** menu and select **Mail Merge**. Click on **Get Data**, then **Open Data Source**, locate your address list and click **Open**.

The data source you just created contains no data records. You can either add new records to your data source by choosing the Edit Data Source button or lay out your main document by choosing the Set Up Main Document button.

Edit Data Source

Set Up Main Document

· 5 · I · 6 · I · 7 · I · 8 · I · 9 · I · 10 · I · 11 · I · 12 · I · 13 · I · 14 · I · 15 · I · 16 · I

Data Form

Title:	Miss
FirstName:	Serena
LastName:	Adams
Address1:	43 Crescent View
Address2:	
City:	Bath
PostalCode:	BA2 3BR

OK
Add New
Delete
Restore
Find...
View Source

Record: |◄ ◄ 1 ► ►|

3 In the 'Create Data Source' dialogue box, you can add, remove or move field names. Arrange them so that they correspond with the information you wish to include in your address list, then click **OK**.
Name your list in the 'Save As' dialogue box. Click **Save**.

New label

If your label type is not listed, you will need to enter the details. In the 'Label Options' dialogue box, click on the **New Label** button and, following the diagram, add the label sizes and give it a name. Click **OK**.

Expert advice

To print a one-off label, or a whole sheet of the same address, go to the **Tools** menu and select **Envelopes and Labels**. Click on the **Labels** tab and type your information into the 'Address Area'. Click the **Options** button, select your label type and click **OK**. Now opt to print a full page of the same label, or just a single label, and click **Print**.

Set Up Main Document

Label Options

Printer information
- ○ Dot matrix
- ● Laser and ink jet   Tray: Default tray (AutoSelect Tray)

Label products: Avery standard

Product number:
- 5096 - Diskette
- 5097 - Diskette
- 5160 - Address
- 5161 - Address
- 5162 - Address
- 5163 - Shipping
- 5164 - Shipping

Label
Details...
New Label...
Type:
Height: 2.51 cm
Width: 6.67 cm
Page size: Letter (8 ½ x 1

Suppress Blank Lines in Addresses
Merge to new document

5 Once you've selected your address list or 'Data Source', Word instructs you to click on **Set Up Main Document**. In the 'Label Options' dialogue box, select the manufacturer from the 'Label products' panel. Scroll down the 'Product number' list and select the correct label. Now click **OK**.

6 The 'Create Labels' dialogue box appears. Click on **Insert Merge Field** and select the fields you want to use in your merge. You may need to insert a space between fields which will appear on the same line, such as 'Title' and 'First Name'. Press the **Return** key for each new line of the address and finally click **OK**.

Create Labels

Choose the Insert Merge Field button to insert merge fields into the sample label. You can edit and format the merge fields and text in the Sample Label box.

Insert Merge Field ▼

Sample label:

«Title» «FirstName» «LastName»
«Address1»
«Address2»
«City»
«PostalCode»

OK   Cancel

Watch out
Before you print the whole list of address labels, it's a good idea to do a test run on plain paper. You only need to print out one page of addresses to check that it is laid out as you want. To do this, click on **Pages** under the 'Page range' section in the 'Print' dialogue box, and type '1' in the panel beside it. Click **OK**. Only your first page of labels will print.

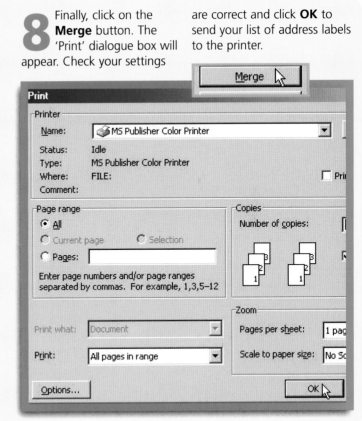

8 Finally, click on the **Merge** button. The 'Print' dialogue box will appear. Check your settings are correct and click **OK** to send your list of address labels to the printer.

7 You can now move on to the third section of the 'Mail Merge Helper' wizard. Click on the **Merge** button. In the dialogue box that appears, click the down arrow beside the 'Merge to' panel and select **Printer**. Check you're happy with the rest of the options.

Use Macros

If you have a particular piece of text or an item, such as a table, that you often use in documents, it makes sense to save it as a macro, instead of creating it from scratch each time. Then, whenever you wish to add that item to a page, you just simply run your macro. A macro can be assigned to a menu, a toolbar, or a combination of keystrokes.

SEE ALSO...
- *Design a letterhead* p 42
- *Edit a toolbar* p 68

BEFORE YOU START
Decide exactly what you want to save as a macro and how you want it to look, whether it is your name and address or a table with a specific number of rows and columns.

1 To create a macro you need to record all of the instructions you would normally use when you are creating your chosen item. These can then be played back instantly, at any time, to recreate it. Go to the **Tools** menu and choose **Macro** then **Record New Macro**. The 'Record Macro' dialogue box will appear on screen.

2 Name the macro, choosing something that reminds you of its function. Under 'Store macro in' you can select 'All Documents' to save your macro in Word's blank document template, or just add it to the document you're working on.

To assign your macro to a toolbar or create a keyboard shortcut for it, click the **Toolbars** or **Keyboard** icons.

3 If you clicked the **Toolbars** icon, you'll see your macro in the 'Commands' panel. Click and drag it onto the toolbar or menu in the main window to which you wish to assign it.

To create a keyboard command for your macro as well, click the **Keyboard** button. Otherwise, click **Close**.

Editing Macros

If you want to change some of the text contained in a macro, go to the **Tools** menu and select **Macro**, then **Macros**. Choose the relevant macro and click the **Edit** button. Any text shown in quotation marks can be highlighted and typed over, as normal.

If you wish to change commands in your macro, it is easiest to delete your macro and recreate it from scratch.

```
Normal - NewMacros (Code)
(General)

Sub InsertClubData()

' InsertClubData Macro
' Macro recorded by mary

    Documents.Open FileName:=""
        ReadOnly:=False, AddToRe
        PasswordTemplate:="", Re
        WritePasswordTemplate:=
    Selection.WholeStory
    Selection.Copy
    ActiveWindow.Close
    Selection.Paste
```

Watch out

Macros can be used to spread computer viruses, so if you open a file created by someone else, and a dialogue box appears, asking whether you want to enable macros, the file could have a virus. The safest option is to not enable the macro and to check the file with your anti-virus software before you open it.

4 In the 'Customize Keyboard' dialogue box, type a keyboard command that will activate your macro into the 'Press new shortcut key' panel – for instance, **Alt + Ctrl + Shift + A**. You can see below whether this command is assigned to another function or not. If it is 'unassigned', click the **Assign** button, then **Close**.

5 The Macro toolbar appears on screen. It is very small and has two buttons – click the left button to stop recording and the right button to pause. Click again on the right button to resume recording.

Create the item that you wish to include in your macro. When it looks exactly how you want it, click the **Stop Recording** button.

6 The next time you wish to add that item to a document, click the toolbar button or menu to which you assigned your macro, or press your keyboard command.

Alternatively, go to the **Tools** menu and click on **Macro**, then **Macros**. In the dialogue box is a list of available macros. Click on your macro and select **Run**.

Sort a list

Word enables you to sort information contained in lists or tables. For example, you may want to make a list of the members of your local club and sort it alphabetically by name. You can also sort by date or number in ascending or descending order, but you need to ensure that you have defined and identified the criteria and format for your sort.

SEE ALSO...

● *Using tables p 48*

BEFORE YOU START
Be aware that if you type a space at the beginning of a word, it will *appear first in the list, as a space comes before 'A' in the alphabet, as do punctuation, symbols or numbers.*

1 To sort a list of names alphabetically, type in the first names followed by the surnames in any order. Press the **Return** key after each entry. When the list is complete, highlight it, go to the **Table** menu, and select **Sort**. In the 'Sort Text' dialogue box, the default setting is to sort your list from A to Z, by the first word of each entry. If this is what you want, click **OK**.

2 To sort your list by surname, click the **Options** button.
Below 'Separate fields at', select the **Other** radio button and type a space in the panel on the right. Click **OK**.

Back in the 'Sort Text' dialogue box, click on the drop-down menu below 'Sort by' and select **Word 2**.
Ensure **Text** is chosen in the 'Type' panel. Click **OK** to initiate the sort.

Bright idea

For easier sorting, convert a list to a table. Highlight the list, go to the Table *menu, click* Convert*, then* Text to Table*. Use the dialogue box to format the table and specify how entries should be separated into cells.*

Watch out

If you want to sort a mixed list by numbers, make sure you specify Number in the 'Type' panel, so that the sort function ignores everything in the list except numbers. If Word sorts your numbers as text, number 1 will be followed by 10, 11, 12 and so on. The number 2 will come after 19!

4 You can choose to sort in ascending or descending order. If you have selected more than one column, you can set the order of your sort – for instance, sorting the data first by column two, then by column three. If you have selected your column headers, click the 'Header row' radio button in the 'My list has' section, so that your headers don't get sorted as well. Click **OK**.

3 If you have a table of information, you can easily reorganise your columns using the Sort feature. Highlight the cells to be sorted, or highlight a whole column by positioning the insertion point at the top of the column and clicking when it changes to an arrow. Go to the **Table** menu and select **Sort**.

Doing a calculation

One of Word's useful features is that it offers some of the functions of a spreadsheet package, such as Excel. It enables you to perform calculations and you can also use formulas in many ways. You can calculate your personal expenditure, develop a table for basic book-keeping or work out a business plan.

SEE ALSO...
- *Using tables* p 48
- *Sort a list* p 92
- *Import & export files* p 96

BEFORE YOU START
You will need an empty row in which to put the formula's result. Position the cursor where you want to insert a row, go to the **Table** menu, select **Insert, Rows above**, then click **OK**.

1 To create a formula to add up a column of numbers in a table, click on the empty cell below the column. Go to the **Table** menu and select **Formula**. The 'Formula' dialogue box appears on screen.

2 The 'Formula' panel says '=SUM(ABOVE)'. This means that it is offering to add up the cells in your column. The equals (=) sign always starts a formula. 'SUM' means addition. '(ABOVE)' means that the formula applies to all the cells above your selected cell.

Click **OK** to activate the formula. The total immediately appears in your table.

3 Alternatively, you can specify a range of cells on which to carry out a function by enclosing them in brackets in the 'Formula' panel. Cells are described using letters for columns and numbers for rows.

Different calculations

You can do more than simple addition in your tables. Here are some of the options available in the 'Paste function' menu: 'SUM' is for addition, while 'MIN' finds the lowest value and 'MAX' finds the highest value.

To multiply values use 'PRODUCT' and to find the number of items in a list use 'COUNT'.

You can round numbers to a specific decimal place using 'ROUND(x,y)' where 'x' is the value and 'y' is the desired number of decimal places.

That's amazing!
You can use the 'AutoSum' button on the 'Tables and Borders' toolbar to add up a column or row of figures automatically. Just click on the empty cell and then on the **AutoSum** button.

4 To use a function other than 'SUM', highlight the cell in which you want the result to appear. Go to the **Table** menu and click **Formula**. This time delete the formula offered to you, leaving the equals sign in place.

5 Click the down arrow beside 'Paste function' to reveal a choice of functions. Scroll down and select **Average** – it will appear in the Formula panel. Now type '(ABOVE)' or type the range of cells between brackets.

You can also choose how the numbers are displayed in your table by clicking the drop-down menu below 'Number format' and selecting one of the options.

6 If you change the formula or any of the figures on which the formula is based, the result will not change until you update the formula. To do this, right-click on the formula cell and select **Update Fields**.

Import and Export files

Importing files into Word from other Microsoft programs, such as Excel and Access, is a good way to present different kinds of information as well as creating an interesting document with lots of visual impact. Likewise, exporting Word files into another program, such as PowerPoint, allows you to display your work in different formats.

SEE ALSO...
- *Save your work p 22*
- *Using tables p 48*
- *Add a picture p 74*

FILE FORMATS AND CONVERTERS

The process of importing and exporting files is not complex. However, certain programs have format restrictions.

Word is primarily a text-based program, whereas Access and Excel are database programs, which means that information is divided into cells, fields and records.

When you import an Access file into Word, you can style it using Word's table formatting options.

However, when you import an Excel table, it is already formatted as a spreadsheet. Once imported, you can only alter its size and where it appears on the page. For the same reasons, you can only export a Word file designed as a table into Access.

Many programs have powerful converters for translating text and images from other file formats. When you try to import a file, your computer will prompt you if it needs to use a converter. If the converters are not installed on your PC, then the program will ask you to install one. Program converters are stored on your Word or Office CD-ROM. Insert the CD in its drive and follow the step-by-step instructions that appear.

IMPORTING FILES INTO WORD

Recent versions of Word let you build multimedia Web pages. As a result, the program recognises and can incorporate many file types in standard documents.

Excel into Word

To insert an Excel worksheet, open a Word document, go to the **Insert** menu and choose **Object**. Select the **Create from File** tab. In the 'File name' panel you will see '*.*', which means 'all files'. Either type the

specific file name over this, or click **Browse** to view a list of your files. Highlight the file to be

inserted and click **Insert**. Click **OK**. Click on a handle and drag to resize the table.

Access into Word

To bring an Access table or query (specified data from a database) into an open Word document, go to Word's **View** menu, click **Toolbars**, then **Database**. On the toolbar, click the **Insert**

Bright idea
The quickest and easiest way to copy small amounts of information from one program to another is to use the 'Cut' and 'Paste' functions, which you'll find in the 'Edit' menu.

Close up
To import an Excel worksheet quickly into a Word document, click the Insert Microsoft Excel Worksheet button on Word's Standard toolbar.

Database button. In the 'Database' dialogue box click **Get Data**, then click and scroll down the 'Files of type' panel at the bottom of the window. Select **MS Access Databases** so you can view available files. Highlight your file and click **Open**. In the 'Microsoft Access' dialogue box, check that

the table or query you require is highlighted and then click **OK** to return to the 'Database' dialogue box.

Choose **Query options** if you want to filter the data by applying a query. This defines exactly which data you want to insert. Click the **Table AutoFormat** button and scroll through the 'Formats' panel to choose a style for your table. Once you have chosen a style, click **OK** to return to the 'Database' dialogue box.

Click the **Insert Data** button. Another dialogue box offers the default choice of 'All' records. Click **OK** to insert the table into your Word document.

As with a table that you create in Word, you can resize the imported table by clicking and dragging on the handles. You can also click in any cell to edit the data it contains, and use the **Table** menu to insert and delete rows and columns (see page 48).

EXPORTING WORD FILES

Specialised programs, such as PowerPoint and Access, vary in the degree of difficulty involved in exporting a Word document into them.

Word into PowerPoint

It is easy to export files from Word into PowerPoint, which is a program for combining text and multimedia for making presentations.

Click on **Open** in the PowerPoint **File** menu. In the 'Open' dialogue box, select **All Files** from the 'Files of type' panel. Locate and double-click

on your Word document. PowerPoint will then automatically convert the document into a format that you can manipulate and make into a professional-looking presentation.

Word into Access

You can import information into Access from Word, but only if you want it to appear in a database format. Therefore, you need to enter the text in the Word document with this in mind. Open a new Word document, type the headings for your records, such as 'Name' and 'Address', and separate each with a comma. Press **Return** before you begin to enter the individual information for each record, also separated by commas. Press **Return** after typing the information for each record. When you have entered all the information, save the document as a 'Text Only' file.

Open Access and go to the **File** menu then **Get External Data**, and **Import**. Locate and double-click on your text file. Make sure the 'Delimited' option is selected in the 'Import Text Wizard' dialogue box, and click **Next**. Click in the 'First Row Contains Field Names' box, and click **Finish**, then **OK**. The information from your Word document will be displayed in a database.

Early versions of Word

If you are sending a file to someone who uses an earlier version of Word, they may have difficulty opening it because of formatting differences. Use the 'Save as' function in the 'File' menu to save it as a file type that is easy to open, such as 'Text only' which removes the formatting. To avoid problems when importing files created in an earlier version of Word, open them using the 'File' menu within Word. In the 'Files of type' panel select the version of Word for the file you wish to open. Word will be able to recognise and open it.

Set up a family Web site

One of the most exciting projects on a PC, if you can access the Internet, is to create your own Web site. It is a great opportunity to trace long lost family members or to promote a club or society to an audience of millions. You can design your site using Word in a matter of minutes, and then connect to the Net and publish your pages.

SEE ALSO...

- *Using tables p 48*
- *Wizards & templates p 50*
- *Add a picture p 74*

BEFORE YOU START
You will need Web space from your Internet Service Provider. To get this, contact your ISP. You will be allocated a few Megabytes of space on their server, as well as a Web address.

2 Select where on the Web page you want the main hyperlinks list to subsequent pages to sit. Click **Next** and add as many pages as you will need – one for each family member, for example. Click **Next** and **Next** again. Click on the **Browse Themes** button to choose a visual theme for the site (you may need to install them from your Office CD-ROM). Click **OK**, click **Next** and **Finish**.

1 With Word running, go to the **File** menu and select **New**. Click the **Web Pages** tab in the 'New' dialogue box. Double-click on the **Web Page Wizard** icon. When the 'Web Page Wizard' dialogue box opens, click **Next**. You can now give your site a name in the 'Web site title' panel. All of your Web site files are stored in the 'Web site Location' folder. Click **Next**.

Install Web Page Wizard

If the 'Web Pages' tab is not shown in the 'New' dialogue box when you open a new blank document (see Step 1), you must install this element of the Word program. Close your programs and insert your Office CD-ROM. Go to the **Start** menu, select **Settings**, **Control Panel**, then **Add/Remove Programs**. Select **Office**, and click **Add/Remove**. In the Office dialogue box, click **Add or Remove Features**, and click the '+' sign beside Office Tools. Click on 'Office Web Components' and click **Update Now**.

Watch out

Some of the dialogue boxes and options shown in the step-by-step may differ slightly from those on your PC. This may be as a result of the options chosen while installing Windows or Office, or caused by software updates received over the Net. However, this will not affect your ability to complete the project.

3 Your styled homepage appears, as does the Frames toolbar. Delete the 'Main Heading Goes Here' text and type your own title in its place. Click on the **Center Align** button. Highlight the title, go to the **Format** menu and select **Font**. Choose a font, style, size and colour. Click **OK**. You can rename any of the hyperlinks listed in the Contents as well as the titles of the sections they are linked to.

4 You need to create columns and rows for your text and images, so click where you want your main text and images to appear. Go to the **Table** menu, select **Insert**, then **Table**. In the dialogue box, select the number of columns and rows you'd like, and click **OK**. Type your text in any of the columns – the height will adjust to accommodate the font size and amount of text.

6 When the image appears, you can adjust it to fit the table. Click on the image and small handles appear in the corners and on each side. Resize the image by clicking on a corner handle and dragging it out to a suitable height or width.

5 Apply a style and size of your choice to the text as before (see Step 3). To insert a picture in a table, click in the column in which you want the image placed. Go to the **Insert** menu, select **Picture**, then **From File**. The 'Insert Picture' dialogue box appears. In the 'Look in' panel, find the folder containing the image you want. Click on the image, then click **Insert**.

Key word
A hyperlink is a feature built in to many sites that allows you to move from one location to another, either on the same Web site or on a completely different Web site, with a single click of the mouse.

Expert advice
To remove a hyperlink from your Web page, highlight the words that activate the link, go to the **Insert** menu and select **Hyperlink**. In the 'Edit Hyperlink' dialogue box, click on the **Remove link** button.

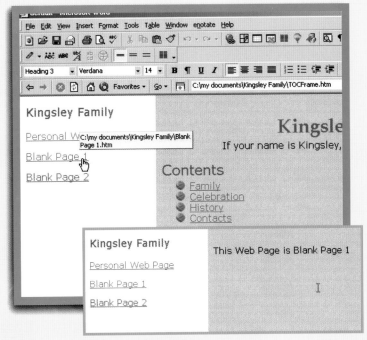

8 You can also create hyperlinks in the text, so that visitors can jump straight to a page that interests them. Highlight the text to be the hyperlink, then click on the **Insert Hyperlink** toolbar button. Click on **Recent Files** and locate the page. Click on the page title, then click **OK**. The hyperlink text is underlined. Click on this, and you will jump to the linked page.

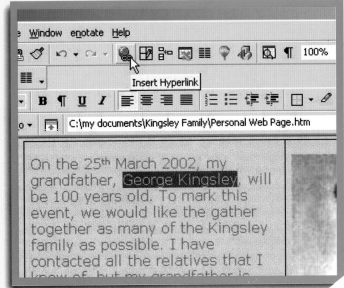

7 When you have finished your homepage, click on one of the 'Blank Page' hyperlinks on the left-hand side. This takes you to a blank page in the style of your homepage, ready for you to work on.

10 To put your pages on the Net, go to the **Start** menu, select **Programs**, then **Accessories**, **Internet Tools** and then choose **Web Publishing Wizard**. Click **Next**, then click on the **Browse Folders** button. Select your Web pages.

9 To create links to other Web sites, type the Web address as part of your text. If it is in the correct Web address format, it will appear as an underlined link. If you don't want the whole address to appear, highlight the text you want to use, and click the **Insert Hyperlink** button. In the dialogue box, type the address in the 'Type the file or Web page name' panel, and click **OK**.

Key word
Copying your Web pages to a server is called uploading *because you are moving documents from an individual computer to a large network. When you* download*, you are doing the opposite.*

Watch out
Make sure you are connected to the Internet before you complete the instructions in Web Publishing Wizard and click on **Finish**. Otherwise the Wizard will not be able to publish your pages online.

11 Click on **Next**. You will be asked for the name of the server to which you are publishing (see Before You Start, page 98). Click on **Next**. Work through the screens, following the instructions and clicking **Next** as you proceed. Finally, click on **Finish**. Click on your home page, then click **OK**. Your pages will now be uploaded.

12 Now open your Web browser and type the Web address for your page into the address box. Click on **Go** (or press the **Return** Key). After you connect to the Web, your homepage will be displayed – just as Web users across the globe will see it.

A

Active window The window in which you are working. To activate a window, click on it and it will jump in front of any other open windows on-screen.

Alignment The position of text and objects on a page in relation to the margins. Text can be aligned to the left or right margin, centred down the middle of the page or justified so that lines of text fit the width of the page, column or box.

Alt key The key to the left of the spacebar on the keyboard that activates a command when pressed in combination with other keys. *See Shift key*.

Arrow keys The four keys at the bottom of the keyboard that move the insertion point up, down, left and right, or allow you to scroll through a window's contents.

AutoFormat This feature is used to apply formatting according to settings that you have created and saved.

Autoshapes A selection of predesigned graphic shapes that you can insert in a document and customize to your needs.

B

Background A colour, texture or image positioned on the page as a layer on top of which all other text and objects sit.

Backspace key This is located in the top right-hand corner of the main block of letter keys on the keyboard, often showing a left-facing arrow. This key deletes text to the left of the insertion point. *See Delete key*.

Bitmap An on-screen image made up of tiny dots or 'pixels'.

Browse (in a window) To search through the contents of your computer, viewing the names of the files in each folder.

Bullet point A small graphic, often a black dot, used to indicate individual statements within a list.

Button An on-screen image on which you can click to perform a function, for example the 'OK' or 'Yes' buttons to confirm an action.

C

Caps Lock Pressing this key will cause all letters that you type to appear as capitals, or in 'upper case'. Press the key again to return to standard characters.

Cell A small, rectangular unit in a spreadsheet, database or table, into which text or figures are entered. Click on a cell to make it active.

Chart A graphic representation of data such as a graph, that can be inserted into a Word document.

Click To press and release the left mouse button once. Menu and dialogue box options and toolbar buttons are selected in this way.

Clip Another word for a ClipArt image. *See ClipArt*.

ClipArt Graphic images that come with the Word program which can be inserted into documents and then resized and manipulated.

Clipboard A virtual location where items cut or copied from a document are stored. The Word Clipboard can store several items of data at a time, regardless of size. Use the Paste command on the Clipboard Toolbar to insert a Clipboard item in a document.

Close A command on the File menu to shut down the active window or document, but not the program. It serves the same function as clicking the 'Close' button in the top right-hand corner of a window.

Copy To make a duplicate of a file, image, or section of a document.

Cursor A marker, usually a flashing vertical line, indicating where text or inserted objects will appear. Also called the 'insertion point'.

Cursor keys *See Arrow keys*.

Cut To remove selected text and/or images to the Clipboard, where they are stored for later use.

D

Database A system for storing data so it can be easily accessed, organized, and sorted. Each entry is called a 'record',and each category in a record is called a 'field'.

Data source A file that contains information stored in database form, such as names and addresses, which can be used in a Mail Merge. *See Mail Merge*.

Default The manufacturer's settings for a program when no others have been specified by the user. For example, Word automatically uses the US dictionary. However, you can change default settings using Options in the Tools menu.

Delete To completely remove a selected file, folder or image, or a piece of text from your document.

Delete key This is located in the group of six keys to the right of the main block of letter keys on the keyboard. This key deletes text to the right of the insertion point. *See Backspace key*.

Desktop The background screen on your PC. It is the starting point for all work. Icons represent various office items, such as files, folders, and a waste basket known as the 'Recycle Bin'. The background is called 'wallpaper', while the Start button gives you access to the programs, your work and the computer's settings.

Destination document The file to which an item currently on the Clipboard is to be added. *See Source document*.

Dialogue box A window that appears on screen when you are using a program. It usually asks for preferences or further instructions to be input by the user in order to complete a procedure.

Digital image A picture that is stored in binary format, so it can be viewed and changed on a PC.

Document A single piece of work created in a program, also known as a 'file'.

Dots per inch (dpi) The number of dots per square inch that either make up an image on screen or that a printer has the capability to print. The more dots, the greater the detail and quality of the image.

Double-click To press and release the left mouse button twice in quick succession. This is most often used to open documents, folders and to activate programs.

Drag A mouse action used to highlight text, reshape objects, or to move an object or file. Click, and keeping the left button held down, move the mouse as required.

Drawing toolbar A supplementary toolbar containing options for adding artistic elements to your Word documents.

Drop-down menu A list of options that appears when you click on one of the headings on the Menu bar.

E

Edit To make a change to an element in a document or to alter the preferences for a program.

End Pressing this key takes you to the end of the line of text on which the cursor is positioned.

Error message A small window on

screen warning that a fault has occurred and, where possible, suggesting an action to remedy it.

Export To save a Word file in a form that allows it to be incorporated in another Microsoft Office application, such as Powerpoint.

External hardware Additional computer equipment attached by cable to a PC, such as a printer.

F

Field A category for information in a database, such as 'Name' or 'Address'.

File Any item stored on a computer, whether it is a program, a document, or an image.

File extension A three or four-letter code assigned to the end of the file name when it is saved. It states the type of file it is so the computer knows in which program to open it. Common extensions are listed here:

File format The way in which files

| Text | .asc .doc .html .msg .txt .wpd |
| Image | .bmp .eps .gif .jpeg .pict .png .tif |

created by different programs are saved. *See File extensions.*

Fill To apply a chosen colour to a designated area. You can also apply a mix of colours using 'Fill Effects'.

Folder An electronic storage location for keeping related files and relevant documents together.

Font A specific style and set of characters for a typeface such as Times New Roman.

Footer A box at the base of every page of a document that contains information relevant to the whole

document, such as page numbers and copyright details. *See Header.*

Format To alter a documents appearance by applying style, typography and layout options.

Form letter A correspondence, created using Mail Merge, which is used to send the same letter to many different addresses .

Formula A set of conditions that carry out a mathematical calculation.

Full Screen This is the view that increases the size of the active window to fill the screen.

Function keys The 12 keys at the top of the keyboard, ranging from F1 to F12, which perform special tasks.

G

.gif file Graphics Interchange Format. A common file format for storing digital images.

Graphic Any type of digital image on a computer, including pictures, photographs and illustrations.

H

Handle The small squares that appear at the corners and sides of an object when you select it. They allow you to adjust the dimensions of the object by dragging them to a different position.

Header Information which appears at the top of each page of a document.

Help key Usually the F1 key on the keyboard, this accesses advice and information on performing a task.

Highlight To select text, images or cells by dragging the cursor over the item. *See Drag.*

Home Pressing this key takes you to the start of the line of text on which the cursor is positioned.

Hyperlink A piece of underlined

text or an object that you click on to take you to a specific Web page using your Web browser (provided you have access to the Internet).

Hyphen A short 'dash' used to join two words, such as that in 'right-hand'. Word also lets you use a non-breaking hyphen. This prevents a hyphenated word from being split when it appears at the end of a line by taking the whole word over to the next line.

I

Icon A graphical representation of a file or a function, designed to be easily recognizable. For example, the printer icon on the Standard toolbar accesses the print function.

Import To bring text, images or files from another program into a Word document.

Indent To position a line or lines of text further from the page margin than the following or preceding lines. Often used to mark the beginning of a new paragraph.

Inkjet printer A type of printer that works by squirting tiny drops of black or coloured ink onto the surface of the paper. Most home printers use inkjets.

Insert To add an element to a document, such as an image or text. This is best done using the Insert menu.

Insertion point *See Cursor.*

Internet Short for 'International Network'. Millions of computers worldwide linked by telephone and cable lines. Users access the Internet via a phone connection to their ISP.

ISP Internet Service Provider. A company that provides a connection for your computer to access the Internet via a telephone line.

Italic A style of writing whereby the letters are typed with a slight slant to

the right. It is most often used to emphasise specific words or phrases, or for the names of books and films.

J

.jpeg Joint Photographics Experts Group. A file format that compresses the data required to make up an image so that it uses less space.

Justify To force lines of text to fit either the space between the left and right margins, or a specified column width.

K

Keyboard shortcut A combination of keys pressed simultaneously to issue a specific command.

L

Laser printer A type of printer that uses a laser to etch images onto a drum and then transfers them to paper, giving a higher quality printout than an inkjet printer.

Layout This refers to the way that items are arranged on a page.

Letterhead A design or information, such as your name and address, that appears at the top of all your letters.

Log on To access a restricted computer, file or Web site using a security procedure, like a password.

M

Macro A series of commands or actions that can be recorded, then activated by a keystroke and played back when required.

Mail Merge A way of incorporating name and address data from another application, such as the Address Book, into Word, allowing you to repeat a letter with the same content but with personalized addresses.

Margins The white space around the edge of the document, the dimensions of which can be adjusted.

Maximize To increase the size of a window so that it covers the entire Desktop area.

Menu bar A toolbar of headings at the top of a program window which displays categorised options in drop-down menus when you click on them.

Minimize To reduce a window to a button on the Taskbar. This allows you to continue running several programs without cluttering the Desktop with windows you are not using at that time.

Modem A device to allow you to connect to the Internet via a telephone line.

Monitor The unit similar to a television which displays all of your work on-screen.

Mouse pointer A small arrow or cursor on screen that moves in relation to the mouse.

Multimedia Computing which combines different methods of communication such as sound, images, text, and video.

My Documents A Windows Desktop icon representing a folder for storing files created by the user.

Net Short for Internet. *See Internet*.

Non-printing characters These are symbols that can be viewed in the document on-screen to show word spacing, paragraphs and line returns. They do not appear on the printed document.

Normal View The default view that appears when you open a

document. You do not see the edges of the page in this view. *See Print Layout and Web Layout*.

O

Object A self-contained item that can be placed in a Word document and retains` its characteristics, such as an image or a spreadsheet.

Office Assistant An animated character who offers suggestions and help as you work in Word. The assistant can be switched on and off, and its settings can be altered to suit the way you work.

Online The status of a computer when it is actively connected to the Internet.

Open To bring a file, folder or program into use.

Orientation An option available when creating a document. Users can choose to set up a page as either Landscape (of greater width than height) or Portrait (of greater height than width), depending on how they want the final document to appear.

P

Page break The position in a document at which one page ends and another begins. Insert a page break manually at any point in a document and Word will reposition the elements on the pages to accommodate it.

Page Setup The settings that allow you to specify the layout of your page, margin sizes, paper size and how you view your document.

Page Up/Page Down These keys take you up or down respectively, to the next page of your document.

Panel A space in a dialogue box in which information can be entered.

Paste To insert text or other data that has been cut or copied to the clipboard.

Pixels Individual dots on a computer screen. The greater the concentration of pixels, the higher the level of detail and improvement in the quality of display.

Point size A standard scale for measuring typefaces. For example, the text on this page is 8 point, whereas newspaper headlines are often 72 point.

Pop-up menu A list of options that appears when you right-click on the Desktop.

Printer driver Software that enables the operating system to communicate with the printer.

Print Layout The document view that shows the page edges so you can see the position of text and objects as you are working. *See Normal View and Web Layout*.

Print Preview The on-screen display of how a document will look when it is printed. Changes cannot be made to the document when using Print Preview.

Properties The attributes of a file or folder, such as its creation date, format and author's name.

R

Radio button A small circle beside an option which you click to activate. An activated option will have a black dot in the radio button.

Range A group of related cells in a table or spreadsheet.

Recycle Bin A Desktop icon and feature used to store files ready for permanent deletion. To delete files in the Recycle Bin, right-click on the Recycle Bin icon and select 'Empty Recycle Bin' from the menu.

Resize To adjust the dimensions of an object in a Word document. Do

this by clicking and dragging the handles that appear on its edges when you select the object.

Resolution The degree of detail on a screen or a printed document, measured in dots per inch (dpi). The higher the dpi, the better the detail.

Return key The large key on the right-hand side of the main block of letter keys on the keyboard. Press to create a new paragraph in your text.

Rich Text Format A way of saving a document so that if it is opened in another word processor or Microsoft program, it will retain the formatting and styling that you applied to it.

Right-click To press and release the right mouse button once. In Word, this causes a pop-up menu of options to appear with different options depending on the item on which you clicked.

S

Save To store or copy a document to a disk, most often a floppy or the hard disk.

Save As This function allows you to allocate a name to a file you are saving. It also lets you save an existing file to a different drive or in an alternative format without affecting the original saved file.

Scroll To move through the contents of a window or menu vertically or horizontally.

Scroll bar The grey panel running either down the right-hand side or along the bottom of a window containing a darker grey block. By clicking on the block and dragging along the panel you can scroll down the page or from side to side.

Search A mini-program that searches for a file, usually by its name or creation date. Also, a command which searches a document for specific information, such as a word or phrase.

Select To click on a file, folder, image, text, or other item, so it can be moved or manipulated.

Server A computer that is the main file storage location connected to a network of other computers. To publish your Web site, you will need to transfer your Web documents from your PC to an Internet server.

Shift key This serves various functions. It can be used to type a capital letter when pressed at the same time as a letter key, or to type the symbols on the number keys, and it can give you access to program functions when pressed together with other keys. For example, pressing 'Shift' + 'Alt' + 'T' together will insert the current time in your document.

Software Programs designed to perform specific functions. For example, Microsoft Word is software designed for word-processing.

Source document The file from which an item is cut or copied to the Clipboard for use in another document.
See Destination document.

Spacebar The wide key along the bottom of the keyboard for inserting spaces between words.

Spellcheck A feature that checks your spelling and suggests corrections. It can use alternative dictionaries to which you can also add terms.

Standard toolbar The line of small icons in Word that sits at the top of the window below the Menu bar and contains common features used when creating word processing documents. These include Save, Print, Spelling and Grammar checker, and Cut, Copy and Paste.

Start The button on the left of the Taskbar for viewing the Start menu.

Status bar The grey bar along the bottom of program windows containing information about the current document.

Style The appearance of the various elements of a document. *See Format.*

T

Tab Short for 'tabulate'. A feature for positioning text at various distances from the left-hand margin.

Tab key The key to the left of the 'Q' key, used to position text at preset intervals across the page. It is also used to move between cells in spreadsheets, or to move from one database field to the next.

Table A group of cells in rows and columns, in which you can type text or place images. Inserting a table in a Word document helps to arrange the elements neatly on the page.

Taskbar The bar usually positioned along the bottom of the screen that displays the Start button, and buttons for programs and documents currently open.

Task Wizard *See Wizard.*

Template A format for saving a document so that its elements can be used as the basis for similar documents.

Text break This feature lets you insert a permanent break between lines of text or paragraphs.

Text only The best way of saving a text document if you want to be able to open it in any other word processor or e-mail program. However, any formatting or styling you applied will be removed.

Themes Background styles that you can apply to your document.

Themes are most effective when used on Web pages as they do not print out on standard Word pages.

Thesaurus An alphabetical list of words and their possible synonyms or antonyms arranged similar to a standard dictionary.

Tile To reduce the size of a group of open windows, arranging them on the Desktop so that they can all be seen at once.

Toolbar A bar or window containing buttons for issuing commands or accessing functions.

Track changes A feature which allows other people to add comments to your document without actually making permanent alterations.

Truetype A fonts file that permits characters to have smooth edges no matter how small or large they appear in a document.

Typeface *See Font.*

U

Undo A function that allows you to reverse the last task or several tasks that you carried out on any individual document.

URL Uniform Resource Locator. The standard style of Internet address for a Website. The main part of the URL – 'www.name.com' – identifies a virtual location for a group of linked Web pages, known as a 'domain'. Any additional parts – '/myhome/mypage.htm', for example – indicate the location of a specific Web page document within the domain. *See Server.*

V

View A menu of options which allows you to change the way a document is displayed on screen.

W

Watermark A feature that alters an image so that it prints as a faint grey background effect behind the text in a document, thus giving the effect of a stationery watermark.

Web Layout The view for working on Web page documents. *See Normal View and Print Layout.*

Window The self-contained viewing and work area of a file or program. Several windows can be open at once on the Desktop.

Windows Explorer A program for viewing the contents of a computer in a single window.

Wizard A program tool that guides users through customizing a predesigned document.

WordArt Text created in a graphic form that can be customized and imported into a document for decorative effect.

Word processing Text-based activites on the computer, such as letter writing. Word processing allows you to create professionally styled documents with an wide range of fonts, sizes and colours.

World Wide Web The part of the Internet composed of millions of linked Web pages that can be viewed using Web browsing software, such as Internet Explorer.

Wrapping The manner in which an object, such as an image, is positioned in relation to text. It can sit behind the text or make the text flow around it in various ways.

Z

Zoom To enlarge an area of a document for ease of viewing.

INDEX

Numbers shown in **bold** type are for main references to the subject listed.

Acknowledgments

We would like to thank the following individuals and
organisations for their assistance in producing this book.

Photography: Karl Adamson

Equipment: Epson, Hewlett Packard, Iomega, IQA, Key Tronic, Labtec

400-109-1